Virtual Foreplay

Comments from relationship experts, authors, spiritual advisors, and dating coaches about *Virtual Foreplay*

"*Virtual Foreplay* will be required reading in my dating course. Eve shows how to effectively transition from cyber dating to face-to-face dating by looking at realistic expectations of love. A must-read for anyone searching for a mate."

— WENDEE MASON, MBA, Founder, DateSmartSingles.com

"The key to successful Internet dating is the ability to present yourself accurately and to translate online friendships into real-world relationships. *Virtual Foreplay* gives singles the skills to make online dating fun and successful."

— Match.com

"Finally, a book from someone who really knows about strategies for successful Internet dating—*Virtual Foreplay!* The web has become one of the best ways to meet someone special—but only if you understand the way the web works. Here are real tips, for safety and for satisfaction, that can help nervous novices and seasoned Internet users avoid dispiriting mistakes. They say that a good guide is hard to find—not any more!"

— PEPPER SCHWARTZ, Ph.D., Relationship Expert, Kiss.com

"*Virtual Foreplay* provides a unique approach to the etiquette of online dating: using the online experience as an opportunity for personal growth! Totally refreshing!"

— Date.com

"Through both practical advice and critical commentary, Hogan does a wonderful job of conveying the mixed blessing that the Internet is vis-à-vis our dating lives. She shows us the opportunities and cautions us on the pitfalls of this exciting new medium. *Virtual Foreplay* is a great tool for anyone interested in finding love online."

—RABBI NILES ELLIOT GOLDSTEIN,
Author of *God at the Edge: Searching for the Divine in Uncomfortable and Unexpected Places*,
Spiritual Advisor to JDate.com.

"*Virtual Foreplay* offers the ultimate preparation to dating online. Asking the questions and doing the exercises will better equip you to create successful relationships—with yourself foremost and then with your sweetheart."

—SUSAN PIVER, Author of *The Hard Questions*

"From the novice computer user to the seasoned web surfer, *Virtual Foreplay* is dedicated to assisting the lovelorn in finding their perfect mate online. It's packed full of practical ideas on how to transition online relationships into the offline world—detailing how to make the experience fun and fulfilling."

—AmericanSingles.com/SocialNet.com

"With the ability to say anything to anyone, anywhere, via the Internet—the questions are: What's worth saying? What's worth knowing? *Virtual Foreplay* is the key to answering these questions in the realm of Internet Dating."

—JOEL ROBERTS, Excellence in Media Coach

"*Virtual Foreplay* is an incredibly practical and powerful guide to finding love on the web. The information, stories, and exercises will help you find the person you're looking for."

—JONATHAN ROBINSON, Author of *Communication Miracles for Couples*

"Cyber-dating neophytes will appreciate Eve Hogan's conversational style and 'true life' stories. *Virtual Foreplay* is a fun and easy read that singles who enjoy online romance will appreciate."

—*The Advice Sisters*, JESSICA B. FREEDMAN and ALISON B. DUNHAM

"An inspiring, motivating and fun-to-read guide to online dating, *Virtual Foreplay* is going to revolutionize the world of online dating and networking."

—ARIELLE FORD, Author of *Hot Chocolate for the Mystical Lover*

"I wish *Virtual Foreplay* had been available when I was dating online! LifePartnerQuest recommends *Virtual Foreplay* and *Intellectual Foreplay* to all of our coaches and clients as essential tools for successful dating!"

—DAVID STEELE, MA, LMFT, CEO and Founder of
LifePartnerQuest Relationship Coaching Resources

"In *Virtual Foreplay,* Hogan skillfully explores the wide-ranging territory of online dating, insightfully presenting both the fun and foibles of the search for that special someone. Taking us beyond the ordinary, she shows us the way to re-connect with our own soul first, opening the door to the kind of deeply honest intimacy that forms the vital bedrock of a healthy love relationship."

—Datingfaces.com

"*Virtual Foreplay*...Online Dating Made Easy! In this fast changing new frontier what more can one ask for?"

—PATRICE KARST, Author of *God Made Easy*,
The Single Mother's Survival Guide and *The Invisible String*

"Internet dating holds great promise as a way to meet your future soulmate, as well as many potential pitfalls. *Virtual Foreplay* helps you chart the waters through this exciting new territory showing you how to maximize your success and overcome the obstacles. Highly recommended!"

—STEFAN GONICK, Psychotherapist, Relationship-Talk.com:
Expert Advice on Love & Dating; SeekingYou.com Picture Personals

"Eve Hogan's *Virtual Foreplay: Making Your Online Relationship a Real-Life Success* is truly the Masters toolkit for making love work online! A 'must have' for online soulmate seekers!

—RENEE PIANE, Author of *Love Mechanics: The Power Tools for Success with Women* and Dating Coach in Los Angeles

"*Virtual Foreplay* is the survival guide to online dating. It is comprehensive, insightful and well written. This labor of love was written from the heart to all of us who struggle to find our special someone, somewhere out there in this great big world."

—DENNIS X. MECCA, Professional Coach

DEDICATION

I dedicate this book to my mom and dad, Meg and Al,
who met on a blind date, had a long-distance relationship,
and are now celebrating their fiftieth anniversary. Thank you
for showing me what unconditional love is all about
and teaching me to see life as a spiritual journey.
I love you more than words can say.

Ordering

Trade bookstores in the U.S. and Canada, please contact:

Publishers Group West
1700 Fourth Street, Berkeley CA 94710
Phone: (800) 788-3123 Fax: (510) 528-3444

Hunter House books are available at bulk discounts for textbook course
adoptions; to qualifying community, health care, and government organizations;
and for special promotions and fund-raising. For details please contact:

Special Sales Department
Hunter House Inc., PO Box 2914, Alameda CA 94501-0914
Phone: (510) 865-5282 Fax: (510) 865-4295
E-mail: ordering@hunterhouse.com

Individuals can order our books from most bookstores, by calling toll-free:
(800) 266-5592 or at www.hunterhouse.com

VIRTUAL
Foreplay

Making Your
Online Relationship
a Real-Life Success

;-)

Eve Eschner Hogan, M.A.

Hunter House PUBLISHERS

Copyright © 2001 by Eve Eschner Hogan

Hunter House Inc., Publishers
PO Box 2914
Alameda CA 94501-0914

Library of Congress Cataloging-in-Publication Data
Hogan, Eve Eschner, 1961-
        Virtual foreplay : making your online relationship a real-life success /
Eve Eschner Hogan.
                p. cm.
        ISBN 0-89793-330-3 (pb)
        1. Dating (Social customs)—Computer network resources. 2.
Man-woman relationships—Computer network resources. 3. Internet. I. Title.
HQ801 .H67 2001
306.7'0285—dc21   2001016620

Project Credits
Cover Design: Jinni Fontana
Book Design and Production: Jinni Fontana
Developmental Editor: Lisa Lee
Copy Editor: Bevin McLaughlin
Proofreader: John David Marion
Acquisitions Editor: Jeanne Brondino
Associate Editor: Alexandra Mummery
Editorial & Production Assistant: Emily Tryer
Acquisitions & Publicity Assistant: Lori Covington
Marketing Assistant: Earlita Chenault
Customer Service Manager: Christina Sverdrup
Order Fulfillment: Joel Irons
Administrator: Theresa Nelson
Computer Support: Peter Eichelberger
Publisher: Kiran S. Rana

Printed and Bound by Publishers Press, Salt Lake City, Utah

Manufactured in the United States of America
9 8 7 6 5 4 3 2 1   First Edition   01 02 03 04 05

Contents

Acknowledgements

As I begin to acknowledge those who helped me with this book, I realize that they are almost all strangers, intimate strangers. Research for this book was done in much the same way as online dating—by dangling a virtual hook to see who would bite. Strangers from all over the world, men and women, gay and straight, young and old, experts and novices, wrote or called to share their experiences with me. I am eternally grateful for the support that you offered by sharing your stories, your pains, and your joys. Thank you, whoever you are; I could not have done this without your heartfelt and thoughtful input. May this book help you to turn your online relationships into real-life successes!

I'd like to acknowledge Ed Orysiek at OtherSingles.com for his amazing and unending interest and support. I look forward to meeting you in person, moving our virtual friendship into the realm of "face-to-face!"

Special thanks also go to Charlotte Nielson, Leanna Harshaw, Kathrin Nolan, Nicole Shubert, and the wonderful crews at Matchnet, Jdate.com, AmericanSingles.com, and SocialNet.com, where I am an online relationship advisor. I'm honored to be a part of the community you are creating. I look forward to more adventures together!

A huge thank you to Jeanne Brondino, Kiran Rana, and the gang at Hunter House Publishers. I not only appreciate and admire you, but love you as dear and lifelong friends. Thank you for your trust, support, encouragement...the list goes on and on.

Thank you to Dennis X. Mecca, a transition coach, who has chatted with me for months, sharing his experiences, stories, and support, and to Marie Agniel, for doing research, sharing stories, and bringing me treats.

To Lauralyn, Ed, Wendy, and Amy Eschner, and Jane and Mike Foley, thank you for listening and laughing and for the special place you hold in my heart.

To my husband and life mate, Steve, I know having a wife who is typing for hours and hours on end is challenging, especially when she is talking with a bunch of single people and checking out online dating sites! You have been nothing but supportive and I deeply appreciate your faith, trust, and love. I love you eternally.

Important Note/Disclaimer

The material in this book is a review of information on approaches to online dating and how to transform encounters begun on the Internet into "real-life" relationships. Every effort has been made to provide accurate and dependable information. The contents of this book have been compiled through professional research and in consultation with professionals.

The skills, tools, and exercises provided in this book are meant to educate the reader and should not be considered a substitute for professional help when warranted. The publisher, authors, editors, and professionals quoted in the book cannot be held responsible for any error, omission, or dated material. If you have questions about the application of the information described in this book, consult a qualified professional.

All names have been changed to protect the identity of the people who participated in the research for this book. Any similarities to real people with the same names is coincidental. All e-mail addresses, usernames, and websites that are used in examples are also fictional and similarity to actual websites, usernames, or e-mail addresses is also coincidental.

Introduction

HEN I MET MY HUSBAND, Steve, I was on vacation with a girlfriend in Hawaii. I saw him sitting alone in a restaurant and felt an instant attraction. I whispered to my friend, "Don't look now, but you've got to see this guy!" Of course, she turned around to look immediately, just as Steve glanced our way. I smiled, embarrassed to be caught staring, as the hostess came to seat us. After watching him for a while, I mustered up some courage, went over to his table, and introduced myself. Fortunately, he was open to talking, and before long my friend and I sat down to join him for the evening. We got together every day for the week of my vacation, until I had to return to California, leaving him on his island home of Maui.

We then embarked on a long-distance relationship. Since this all took place just prior to the boom of the Internet and e-mail, we spent hundreds of dollars each month talking on the telephone, getting to know each other better. We decided that neither of us wanted to go through the hassle of moving and redesigning our lives to include the other, unless we were fairly sure we were making the right choice in a life partner. So, we began asking each other many questions and listening carefully to the answers with the intention of making sure that we were, indeed, a match.

As we asked and answered these questions, one evening I became acutely aware that, aside from some of the "basics," I wasn't sure what I really needed to know about Steve before I made the commitment to be with him. I went to work the next day and asked

1

everyone I encountered, "What do you need to ask someone before you get seriously involved?" hoping to come up with a few questions to ask him that night on the phone. Much to my surprise, everyone had his or her own idea about what I should ask! Everything from practical household issues to deep philosophical questions, from child-rearing values to questions about sex was covered—I added these to a list that quickly grew into the hundreds. I couldn't wait to talk to Steve so I could share all the questions I had gathered. Our phone bills grew even larger, as we dove into the multitude of new things we had to talk about!

Somewhere in the middle of our discussions, we concluded that if we needed help figuring out what to ask before getting more seriously involved, other people would benefit from our "research" as well. We continued gathering and compiling more questions, testing them on each other, and categorizing them for practical use. Out of this process, our book *Intellectual Foreplay: Questions for Lovers and Lovers-to-Be* was born. *Intellectual Foreplay* presents the questions we gathered as a useful tool for guiding people to use their heads, while paying attention to their hearts, before sharing their lives.

As an educator and facilitator of self-esteem and communication workshops for parents, teachers, students, and the public, I began incorporating these concepts into my workshops, and, as time passed, I specialized more and more in human relationships—whether family, business, or personal. After I had been teaching skills for building healthy relationships for some years, the Internet became a reality, adding a whole new dimension to dating. More and more of the couples I encountered had first "met" each other online.

Interviewing and guiding people about their relationships, both online and off, I became fascinated with the phenomenon of online dating and its implications in terms of our ability and inability to connect. The Internet opened up the whole world as our social playground, allowing us to look for a spouse, partner, or friend from the comfort of our own homes. I have since become an online relationship advisor, helping people to sort out their virtual relationships and bring them to fruition. And online dating, which started out as an activity few people would admit to participating in, has grown into something almost everyone has had some experience with whether directly or indirectly. On the Net, more than before, the value of communication and the art of intellectual foreplay is vital to establishing healthy relationships. Out of this union of technology and intimacy, *Virtual Foreplay* was born.

As I was talking with a friend about *Virtual Foreplay,* she asked me why anyone would need to go online to meet people. She added, "Aren't they just a bunch of geeks?" I laughed, saying that hers was a common misconception because online dating has been almost a secret society. People often don't talk about it unless they are asked. I explained that some of my most respected and interesting friends were logging in online to meet people; they were not geeks at all. I went on to say, "You live alone. If you feel like going out one night but don't really want to do the bar scene, or none of your friends are available, you can just turn on your computer and meet people. It's a fun alternative to going out and more interactive and social than watching TV. In the process, you might connect with someone you would like to meet in person." A light bulb went on for her: this was more than antisocial people looking for love.

There are many generalizations floating around about online dating but, just like anything else, online dating is what we make of it. The Internet is a *technology*. How we use that technology and our experience with it are as individual as the people you'll find there. And they are *all* there—the good, the bad, the young, the old, the funny, the strange, the rich, the poor, the single, the married, and the wonderful.

People—*normal* people—are reaching out on the Internet simply to socialize. It has become a form of entertainment, akin to watching TV or reading a book. One woman, a single mother, explained to me that online dating allowed her to socialize and meet new people while staying home with her kids. Another woman said, "It's become a new hobby for me." Much like fishing, you throw your bait in the water, so to speak, and see what comes up in the Net—Internet, that is!

This technology has introduced, or rather magnified, a need for some new skill sets. Not only do we need to be able to type, spell, and punctuate, but we need to establish a new etiquette, or "e-tiquette." This etiquette is also being defined for other long-distance relationships, which are becoming more common as people with busy lives spread out across the globe. Now, it is not unusual to hear of couples who are married but live in different cities. Both online dating and long-distance relationships require the ability to express ourselves verbally, to establish our comfort zones and boundaries, to define appropriate and inappropriate virtual behavior, and, perhaps most challenging, to align our virtual selves with our real selves to ease the transition from one to the other.

The Full Spectrum

Virtual Foreplay is a guide to help you use the process of dating as a tool for self-discovery, and bring true love into your life while meeting and mating on the World Wide Web. This is not just another look at "how to date on the Internet." There are other books of "do's and don'ts" and websites full of free advice for those who simply wish to try it. Instead, *Virtual Foreplay* is a guide for Internet users on how to transform their virtual encounters into satisfying and fulfilling real-life relationships.

The world of Internet dating is a mirror that shows us an image of ourselves, our society, and our interpersonal skills. Both the good and the bad are spotlighted, allowing us to view them clearly. Online dating has many of the same elements that dating in the physical world has, but some things that are subtle or camouflaged in face-to-face dating are more likely to be "in your face" and explicit in online dating. The anonymity that is possible online gives us a certain boldness that we may otherwise lack. People online are often more blunt and to the point. It is easier both to speak the truth and to tell lies when you aren't looking another person in the eyes. By taking a step back, examining our own mirrored image, and determining what our interactions reveal, we can move toward creating greater intimacy and healthier relationships in our lives.

Some of the benefits of online dating include:

* bringing us a greater sense of confidence
* enhancing our communication skills
* reawakening our intense desire for intellectual intimacy
* verifying the value of asking questions and getting to know each other deeply
* reinstating a sense of romance into our hearts
* emphasizing the value of being honest about who we are
* clarifying what we want and what we don't want in relationships
* providing the ultimate safe sex
* giving us a tremendous sense of abundance and choice

The Internet has provided us with a great way to meet new people; however, *meeting* isn't the only element necessary to create and maintain real-life relationships. Many people who are confident, communicative, and outgoing *online* are at a loss as to how to transfer these qualities to their face-to-face relationships. They experience virtual intimacy and companionship but in their daily lives may feel awkward and alone.

If loving, supportive, real-life relationships are what you seek, contact on the Internet can be the "virtual foreplay" to such wonderful connections. *Virtual Foreplay* will show you how to look at the way you interact with others online and apply the interpersonal skills you hone there to *all* of your relationships, recreating in your daily life the depth and intimacy that you are enjoying online. Through applying what we learn online, we have the ability to create a more honest, compassionate, risk-taking, confident society. The Internet has also given us an opportunity to reach out worldwide, allowing us to learn about other people and their customs. This alone, if handled mindfully, has the potential to bring more acceptance and understanding to the world.

With every beneficial technology, there is always risk. The anonymity of the Internet has also brought with it:

* an increased opportunity to be dishonest
* an ease in hurting people through cruelty or dismissal
* a temptation to be unfaithful in our existing relationships
* an opportunity to live in a fantasy world without a base in reality
* a superficiality about what is important
* a disassociation from the consequences of our behavior and the power of our words

If we, as individuals, move forward with this technology without paying any attention to where we are heading, we may find that we are creating a virtual world with a virtual intimacy that will leave us feeling more empty than full. We risk the possibility of spreading more isolation, loneliness, deception, and pain.

Our lives are made up entirely of relationships—with our parents, children, siblings, coworkers, bosses, clients, sweethearts, and lovers, as well as with strangers. If we continuously distance ourselves from others and focus on self-gratification, without having people who look us in the eye, hug us and hold us, we risk doing harm to others—even more than we already have.

Being connected, having a sense of belonging, is one of our core needs. The Internet and online dating can be magnificent tools for bringing more connection into our lives, but they must be used consciously, or we will only be fooling ourselves. We'll be left totally unable to re-create the connection with other people *offline,* in the territory of our daily interactions.

Because this technology offers a full spectrum of opportunity, from the relationship-enhancing to the relationship-destroying, online interaction requires that we make a conscious choice about what we want to create in our lives, that we align our behavior with our goals, and that we take responsibility for creating healthy relationships.

We need to have the tools to transition from the virtual to the actual, so that we can experience intimacy and connection in every facet of our everyday lives. By reading *Virtual Foreplay,* you will gain the skill of self-observation and the power to make choices. You will also learn to align your virtual self with your physical self, thereby creating wholeness in your being, rather than fragmentation. *Virtual Foreplay* will lead you toward finding your *soul,* as well as your *mate,* enabling you to connect with others in a deep and meaningful manner.

As Julie, a 31-year-old woman, shares, "By dating online, I grew emotionally and learned more about myself through the process of having to describe myself to total strangers. This method of dating forced me to look at myself through other people's eyes and I saw myself in a different light. After meeting several people, I realized the misconceptions we have about ourselves. I know myself better now." This is a powerful starting point for building a relationship with someone else. Sylvia, 27, had a similar eye-opening experience dating online. "When people write down what they feel and think, they learn a lot about who they are. As I recently read in a book, 'I didn't know I had that thought until I spoke it...' or as I add—*write* it. Writing and speaking about oneself is necessary for self-growth."

Virtual Foreplay will benefit not only those of you who are dating online, but also those who are curious about this phenomenon and want to know more, and those who are vicariously dating online via their friends' shared e-mails and stories. For the millions of people participating directly, there are millions of family members and friends trying to understand what their loved ones are going through while being called upon to counsel them through the process. *Virtual Foreplay* can help those people offer healthy support.

What Is Virtual Foreplay?

According to Webster's, *virtual* means "not actual, but equivalent; being in essence, not in fact." It is a strange word that leads us to think of "almost, but not quite." Virtual dating is dating in essence, but not in actuality. It includes an illusion or fantasy dimension that generally leads us to the reality, but not necessarily and not right away. Unfortunately, there are many times when the fantasy and the reality don't ever converge, which, in the world of Internet dating, can be frustrating, deceiving, and time-consuming.

Looking at yourself in a mirror is a virtual look at yourself. It isn't exactly the same as looking at the real you, but it is an equivalent. Your online presentation of yourself as a potential partner or life mate isn't exactly you either; it is a virtual version of you. (Some representations are more equivalent than others.) Hence, the intrigue and desire—the foreplay to a relationship—that can be created via online dating isn't necessarily realistic either. If you don't accurately represent your image, you'll get people falling in love with the *virtual* you and falling out of love when they meet the *real* you.

So, where does the foreplay come into all this? In the physical realm, foreplay is the stimulating interaction that comes before sexual intercourse, the tantalizing touch that creates readiness for more. Online—or virtual—foreplay is the stimulating interaction that determines whether there will be an entwining of two lives, but it is done with words rather than touch. Communicating with depth and hope, sharing intimacy—even via something as seemingly impersonal as e-mail—is like the foreplay *to the foreplay,* if you will. After all, it is foreplay in essence, if not in actuality, and may eventually lead to the real thing somewhere down the road.

Foreplay also enters into all of this because there is a lot of virtual sexual activity taking place on the Internet. Many people are reaching out via e-mail, chat rooms, and websites to add a new dimension to their sex lives. Because this is such a new phenomenon, people are struggling with how to make sense of cyber sex, or "cybering" as it is often called. Differing opinions abound as to what is and what isn't *really* sex. To date, there hasn't been anything in our societal moral code that covers "sex before meeting" and its impact on our relationships. In Part I of *Virtual Foreplay,* we will look at this topic more closely and examine what it can mean to you.

There is another aspect of online dating as virtual foreplay that may not be as obvious. Something about encountering a person who is confident, enthusiastic, self-respecting, and aware is immensely attractive. Putting yourself out there for anyone to view and critique or lust after takes a certain amount of guts. Dating online sounds like fun until you realize that you have to tell someone about yourself in a way that is honest yet intriguing, within a limited space. For some, this process of increasing and expressing self-awareness is more challenging than meeting people face-to-face.

The initial stages of online dating all take place over the computer, without the benefit of being able to flash a winning smile. When people are faced with the prerequisite questionnaire for being listed on a dating site and are challenged to describe their best qualities in a unique and interesting way, many are confronted with deep-seated issues of low self-esteem or shame. This can be painful, making it easy for them to give up after a couple of disappointments or slow starts. But to let an experience so rich with opportunities for growth and companionship slip by would be the real shame. Those who actually go through the effort to put themselves online, answer questions about themselves, and field inquiries from strangers will find that their confidence and self-esteem can grow immensely from the process.

Soul Mates

I should disclose right from the start that I don't believe in the concept of a "soul mate." I believe, instead, in soul *mates*—plural. I have seen many people lose a partner to death or divorce and feel totally lost, as if there were no one else out there for them. In reality, it was just a matter of time before they were able to find another life partner, one with whom they shared a similarly deep connection, if not a deeper one. How cruel and sad it would be to have a life with only one possibility for true love on a planet with billions of people. That is quite a hit-or-miss proposition. In reality, we are able to feel a deep, soul-to-soul recognition with more than one person. Who we choose as our life partner can indeed be *a* soul mate, but need not be our *only* soul mate.

A soul mate is one whom our soul knows and has agreed to meet with body-to-body in life. Our heart intuitively feels an immediate connection when it recognizes one of our soul mates. In the movie *The Highlander,* there are immortals wandering around among the regular people. Whenever an immortal is in close proximity to another immortal, they can feel the other's presence. It works the same way with soul mates. Sometimes it is just a glance, a feeling, or a chemistry that is familiar or recognizable.

We have free will and so do other people. Consequently, the path a soul mate takes in their life may not be in alignment with the path we have chosen to take in ours. It is then that our heads have to get involved, to be sure we are making the right choice of a soul mate as our life partner. Monogamy is a matter of *choice,* not lack. We are faithful to our life partner not because there is only one person that we are attracted to or that we can love, but because we have chosen to be monogamous with them.

The goal of *Virtual Foreplay* is to enable you to find the soul mate of your choice online and to have the skills for creating and maintaining the love of your life offline. More important than finding friends, a romantic partner, or life mate, this book will guide you to find your self, your soul, and your passion. It will help you put your best foot forward when you present yourself on the World Wide Web, rather like polishing your soul, letting it shine through you vibrantly, to assist your soul mates in recognizing you, too. With or without a mate, aligning with one's own soul is a powerful way to live.

By working through the material in *Virtual Foreplay*, you will be guided to look at yourself from a different perspective. From there, you can evaluate whether your values, dreams, and goals are adequately defined and expressed. *Virtual Foreplay* will then lead you toward aligning the virtual you with the actual you. This preparation, by increasing the confidence-, esteem-, and awareness-building potential of online dating, will send you into the arms of a newly met mate with the skills and the strength that can create a real-life success.

In *Intellectual Foreplay*, I emphasize the importance of aligning your values with those of your partner. In *Virtual Foreplay*, the attention is placed on aligning your virtual presence with your real essence and using the experience as a process for growth. With *Intellectual Foreplay* and *Virtual Foreplay* working hand in hand, you'll be well equipped with the tools you need for creating the love of your life.

Browsing This Book

I'm sure you are familiar with the term "You can't see the forest for the trees," implying that when you are in the midst of things, it is harder to see what is really going on—the big picture. One of the reasons we go to counselors or talk to friends about our difficulties is because, if the counselor is any good, he or she mirrors back to us what he or she is seeing so that we can see it, too. Seeing our own situation filtered through different eyes gives us a new perspective, which allows us to make different decisions than we would have otherwise made. We can, however, learn to see ourselves through "different" eyes without always having to bounce things off of another person. Larry, a 30-year-old, explained, "I've learned about my personality and my best qualities from online dating. I know more about what I'm looking for out of life, and who my ideal partner is."

Online dating can be an excellent tool for reflecting back to us the areas in which we excel, as well as areas in which we may need to make new choices. If we pay attention, it reveals to us aspects of our personality that we may want to build on or enhance, and it defines our character, as well as clarifying what we are looking for in a partner.

As you read *Virtual Foreplay*, you will be guided to see long-distance relationships or online dating as "the forest" (rather than a jungle!), and your personal experiences with it as "the trees." By looking at the forest from above, you will be able to choose the paths and trails that will get you through it safely, with ease and grace. Not only will you gain skills for creating healthy relationships, you'll also greatly enhance your likelihood of obtaining a successful match.

Interspersed throughout the book, you will find questions to ask yourself to help you to better identify your thoughts, beliefs, and behaviors, enabling you to choose new ones if necessary. I highly recommend that you answer these in a notebook or journal. What you discover about yourself and the words that you choose to use will serve you as you fill out online dating questionnaires or answer questions posed to you by a prospective partner.

Virtual Foreplay is divided into six parts. The first part, **Cyberspace—To Boldly Go Where We Have Never Gone Before,** will give you a look at the world of dating and how it has changed over the last century. The issues of sex and love online, or over long distances, will be examined and some thought-provoking guidelines will be shared. Since there are really no established rules for how all of this works, you will be guided to determine your own personal code of ethics for navigating these new avenues of dating.

Part Two: Putting Yourself on the Line will invite you to look at yourself as if you were creating a website in which you were the product. This process requires sincere self-observation and self-consideration, as you determine who you are and what you want to reveal about yourself. By participating in the exercises found in this section, you will decide what is important about yourself and whom you want to attract. You will also become better equipped to answer challenging online questionnaires, presenting your virtual self in the most positive and accurate light. The focus of this section will be on shining a light that allows you to see your *process with dating* as a wonderful opportunity to create value in your life from even the most difficult experiences.

Part Three: Making Contact will turn the spotlight from you toward your interactions with others. By practicing intellectual foreplay online, you will discover how to ask the right questions, pay attention to the answers, and determine the right partner for you—one whose values and goals are in alignment with your own.

Part Four: The Black Hole of Cyberspace will lead you through the dark side of dating online and offline—handling emotional emergencies. The root of the word *emergency* is "emergence"; hence, in this section you will gain some useful tools for turning any seemingly disastrous situation into the emergence of something greater. You will explore and conquer the danger of projections, rejections, and assumptions.

In any long-distance relationship, the transition from *technically* being together to *actually* being together brings with it several challenges, which **Part Five: Moving from Virtual to Physical** will address. The sudden necessity to share a home, chores, and space is one consideration, but even the change in communication from virtual to verbal can be a challenge. When we are self-observant and responsive, we are better able to make these transitions without compromising our values. Respect is the key issue, both for yourself and for your partner.

One aspect of the forest-for-the-trees aspect of online dating that becomes visible when we pull back a little is that never in our lifetimes have we had a more awesome opportunity to network the world round.

Part Six: Love Is a Universal Language addresses the bigger picture of online dating, which undoubtedly will soon simply become online *networking*. Why not expand what we are seeking; why not go beyond personal relationships to include relationships of all kinds? In order to reach out globally with such a powerful tool, we need to be conscious and responsible. We are the custodians of each other's hearts and need to take responsibility for the impact that we are capable of having in the world.

Personal relationships online can be looked at as a model. How we use this technology, how we treat each other, the integrity that we display, and what we gain from the experience can be transitioned into the many, many other reasons for reaching out to the world on the Internet. In the big picture of things, online dating is just the "virtual foreplay" of what is yet to come!

Author's Note

While writing, I've discovered a few challenges in using the English language, and I would like to point them out from the start. The first is not having any word that is singular for someone who could be male *or* female. In an effort to avoid constantly writing "he/she" or "his/her," I have used "them," "they," or "their" to refer to a singular person, although this use is not actually grammatically correct.

The other challenge I found is that there is a tendency for us—myself included—to refer to the world *offline* as the "real" world, or "in my real life," when in actuality, *all* of our time is spent in our real life, in our real world. The Internet is part of our reality now, and our time in front of a computer is real time spent. Our words, even if e-mailed, are real thoughts that have a real impact on the recipient. If I imply in my writing that it is not the case, it is merely done because it makes contrasting the virtual world of cyberspace with the physical world of concrete space more easy and convenient. I considered referring to our face-to-face relationships as our "*real*ationships," but I figured that would get old before long.

One other concern that I'd like to address is that I've noticed an inequality between the many "bad" stories that circulate about online dating and the "good" stories in my book! I want to stress that success stories about people who have met online and are joyfully sharing a fulfilling relationship are every bit as prevalent as the more disappointing stories. Every online dating site has a huge compilation of success stories for you to read. However, the majority of the stories I gathered were from people who were still dating online. People who have married their online mate are, for the most part, no longer accessible via the online dating websites where I interviewed people. Rather, they are at home in the midst of their real-life relationships.

In addition, *Virtual Foreplay* is about taking the experiences that you have, learning from them, and turning them into a stimulating step forward. Most people do not need help doing this with their successes—although some do! Rather, it is the hard knocks that we need help making sense of and from which we learn so much. I reiterate, online dating is a rich and fertile ground for discovery about one's self and one's potential mate.

PART ONE

Cyberspace—To Boldly Go Where We Have Never Gone Before

"Having worked in the 'Singles Industry' for the last 13 years, I have seen many avenues for meeting people (personal ads, dating services, social groups) come full circle from a totally unacceptable and 'scary or desperate measure' to 'you mean you've never used a dating service?' The Internet is the meeting place of this decade for single people and will continue to be so for several years."

KELLY HOWARD, EDITOR AND PUBLISHER OF *SINGLEFILE* MAGAZINE

"I have always had low self-esteem. From dating online, I learned that I am a good-looking person, and this really built up my confidence. When you send photos out and get nothing but positive responses, that makes you feel self-confident and it helps you in your day-to-day real world."

JACQUELINE, 32

"I've learned that sooner or later I have to take a chance to meet someone."

HENRY, 41

"I have met guys who I might not have even talked to if we had met in person, but because we developed a relationship, a friendship, on the Internet first, we were able to continue on and have a wonderful relationship. I've found that someone who I might not think is all that attractive becomes attractive once I've gotten to know what a great guy he is; and by contrast, I've met men who I thought were really handsome until I got to know them, and then they looked ugly."

MELISSA, 38

1

Shifting Times

G INA WAS WAITING FOR A BUSINESS ASSOCIATE in a restaurant where they were meeting for dinner. She had arrived first, informing the hostess that she was expecting someone and asking her to please direct her friend to the table. After a few minutes a man slid into the booth across from her, smiled, and said, "Hi, I'm xyz@server.com." Tina looked at him blankly, trying to figure out what that had to do with her, when suddenly she realized that Mr. xyz@server.com was on a first-time cyber date and he didn't know whom he was meeting. She laughed and said, "Sorry, I'm not who you think I am. I'm actually waiting for a coworker. The hostess must have sent you to the wrong table." "Too bad," he said. "So, what's *your* e-mail address? Perhaps we can meet another time!"

As recently as 10 years ago, few of us would have believed that we would be looking for love on a computer. Now, literally millions are turning to the Internet to meet friends, lovers, or a potential spouse. And, whether they've tried online dating or not, it seems everyone has an opinion about this modus operandi. Every time I mention "Internet dating," I receive one extreme response or another, shared either with glee or with a groan.

One woman told me that her sister's husband of several years had disappeared with a woman he met online. "One day she went into his computer to get something and found the e-mail that set up the meeting time and place. She then started reading other e-mail, only to find the follow-up letters that shared some of the intimate details of their sexual encounter. He left my sister for his online lover. She was devastated." Other people shared similar stories about men and women leaving their partners for their online lovers.

For every sad story, however, I also hear many happy ones. One man told me, "My friend met her husband that way and they are a perfect match! She swears by online dating!" Another shared, "It was so funny! Two of our friends, Sasha and Jacob, called us on the same day to tell us about the wonderful person they had met online. Jacob didn't realize that we knew Sasha and she didn't know that we knew Jacob! Now we are all going out together and they are so perfect for each other!"

This new dating technology is both a blessing and a sign of some pretty interesting social transitions. The blessing is that millions of people are finding a way to reach out to others and connect. Success stories abound; it isn't at all uncommon to encounter happy couples who met on the Internet. The other side of the blessing is that many of those millions of people are lonely and are, for numerous reasons, having a hard time finding a life partner in the course of their daily lives. Millions of people are looking for love and they are doing it very differently than they ever did before.

Dating has changed dramatically over the last few centuries. Not that many years ago, we depended on our village matchmaker, a minister, or our parents to make a match. At the very least, our parents' and society's approval were a critical part of our choice of partners, and we took their wishes into careful consideration. As recently as the 1940s and 1950s, society's approval was still pretty important, and since it wasn't socially acceptable to be having pre-marital sex, as soon as a teenager's sex drive kicked in, they started aiming for marriage. It was expected that everyone would grow up, get married, and have kids, and starting the process just out of high school was a pretty common practice. In those days, people also took their marriage vows seriously and intended to stay together through thick or thin—like it or not.

In the 1960s and 1970s, we struck out for independence. Women started seeking careers, choosing not to have children—or waiting to have them—and "free love" became a powerful movement. Many people were seeking freedom, and, at least in the west, sexuality was one of the ways we expressed our ability to make choices. Many of us no longer waited to get married to have sex (or to admit that we were having it!). Divorce became more prevalent as people realized that they could go against the "system" and leave marriages that didn't serve them. We also began living together, rather than getting married, in greater numbers.

As we entered the 1980s, our choices in partners also became part of our rebellion, as we sought to marry for love regardless of society's approval. The barriers of race, religion, age, and sexual orientation began to fall like the Berlin Wall. The divorce rates continued to climb, sending millions of divorcees back into the dating world. In addition, as our life span increased with new medical technology, we had greater numbers of older and widowed singles looking for love. For many of these older singles, all the "rules" of dating had changed or disappeared since they had gone through the process the first time.

Then AIDS hit, knocking the free love movement backward and making us all calm down our hormones a bit. Concern about safe sex led us back to thinking about the benefits of monogamy. With this came an increased demand for new ways to meet other singles in search of mates and a desire for rules or guidelines for making relationships work.

By the 1990s, choice of partners had become almost entirely up to the individual. We were, and are, meeting and marrying across all political, gender, religious, and racial boundaries—with the Internet making these boundaries almost nonexistent. Physical distance is now practically the only thing that stands between us and people from anywhere else across the world.

Can you imagine, now in the new century, your father coming home and informing you that he and his business associate had shaken hands on a marriage between you and an associate's son or daughter? It is an unfathomable concept for most of us. And yet, with all the freedom that we have demanded, it is interesting to take a step back and see how we have done for ourselves.

As we look at the general trend toward making our own dating choices, we see another interesting trend that has simultaneously developed. The current divorce rate is around 50 percent, which is a pretty strong indicator that something isn't working too well. In a gamble, fifty-fifty odds aren't very encouraging—and I shudder to think what the "unhappy marriage" rate must be! Statistics like this one don't leave the impression that we've been doing such a good job.

If we want full freedom to choose our own life partners, we simultaneously need to take full responsibility for our choices and for advancing our interpersonal skills to a level that contributes to creating—and maintaining—the love of our lives. Ultimately, it makes no difference who we choose as a partner, if we ourselves do not have the interpersonal skills to support and maintain a relationship. Even if we find the mate of our dreams, we still need to be the mate of *their* dreams, as well.

The Lonely Planet

Many times I have heard the Earth referred to as the "lonely planet," and I always thought it just meant that, as far as we knew, we had the only planet teeming with life on it. With so many people capable of generating so much love, it never occurred to me that this is a planet of *lonely people*. Among those who are single, married, young, or old, loneliness is rampant. A few years back, there was a study done in which researchers asked thousands of single people what their biggest complaint was, to which the majority answered, "loneliness." The researchers then asked thousands of married people the same question and the majority also answered, "loneliness." Being married or in a partnership isn't what creates a sense of connection with others—rather, it is your interpersonal skills and your ability to make wise choices and to establish intimacy within relationships.

There is no need to be lonely on a planet with billions of other people. It is a matter of choice. We can be in a room full of people day in and day out and still not feel connected. We can ride in an elevator less than a foot away from another person without making eye contact and saying, "Hello." We can pass hundreds of people on the street without really seeing any of them. We can turn down opportunities to stretch our comfort zones and meet new people. We can stay on our computers, interacting only with the words and pictures on the screen. Or, we can choose to connect with others and tap into the many opportunities for deep and satisfying relationships.

In order to do this, however, we need to raise our self-esteem, reach out to others, let down the walls between us, and allow love to roam the planet. Now, with the World Wide Web at our fingertips, we have the capability of sending that love and connection from country to country, person to person, almost instantaneously. The new technology of e-mail and the Internet has allowed us to connect with people in a whole new way, but it is also one or two steps removed from direct contact. In order to be successful at creating true connections—virtual or otherwise—we have to be able to take responsibility for the quality we are creating in our relationships. In order to connect with others, we first must be able to connect with ourselves. In order to find our soul mates, we must first find our own souls!

How do you reach out to others? Do you take advantage of opportunities to connect with people or do you create a sense of loneliness?

What's All the Hoopla About?

Back in the good old days, people used to communicate with letters. Many of us can remember the hopeful excitement when the mailman arrived. Even today, when there is a personal letter in a box normally full of bills and advertisements, it is a thing to behold! E-mail has brought back the written word as a means of communication. We are rediscovering our ability to express ourselves verbally, committing our thoughts to writing. There is something about someone's taking the time to write, composing and sending their thoughts, that feels more meaningful, more of an investment, than if they were to just pick up the phone to call.

The Internet and e-mail have also restored a sense of romance that has contributed greatly to their huge success in enrolling so many people. With the resurgence in written communication has also come the resurgence of the *love letter.* A friend of mine, Sylvia, showed me an e-mail a man had sent in response to her profile that was complete with a digital image of a rose. In his next letter, he sent a picture of a butterfly along with his note—virtual romance at its finest. While a picture of a bottle of wine at sunset would hardly serve the traditional purpose, it is fun to find creative ways to send special messages to the one you are courting. And, when you have no idea how many suitors your potential sweetheart may have online, it behooves you to find ways to make your e-mail stand out!

Jim, an acquaintance of mine who has been dating online for years, printed out his online profile for me to read. I was impressed with the depth he shared in just a few paragraphs. He talked sincerely about things any woman would want to hear: romance, simplicity, spirituality, and soul-to-soul connection. I found it striking that, while I had not known him a long time, I had known him *in person* and yet been unaware of many of the aspects of his personality that his profile revealed. Reading his words offered a much deeper look at what mattered to him and what he thought about.

Then Jim offered to let me read several of the responses that women had sent him. I felt a little voyeuristic, as if reading a romance novel. I was privy to these women's heartfelt words, poured out hopefully to this man they had never met. They shared their deepest desires, their past pains, and they asked to be given a chance. As I felt my own heartstrings being pulled, I realized, once again, the powerful draw of deep, meaningful, and honest communication. Indeed, sharing who you are with someone and listening to their responses is very stimulating. We, as a society, are generally starved for this kind of communication and connection with other people. We want intimacy that goes beyond the physical, yet excluding the physical isn't satisfying either. The Internet can provide a wonderful ground on which to practice this kind of meaningful interaction, but we need to take those skills into our physical world, opening our hearts and souls to the people in our daily lives as well.

The Internet has also reinstated a sense of hope in our society. As Miki, a woman in her 40s, said, "By dating online, I learned that I am not the only person in the world searching for someone special to be a part of my life." The Internet has shown people that they are not alone. With so many profiles, so many available people looking for partners, the Internet has also revealed that there truly are many opportunities. Whether online or off, with a little persistence, you can meet some very interesting people. Among all those available, surely the right one is out there looking for you, too!

Time Is More Valuable Than Money

The online dating world is like a candy store for those who are searching for love. It is a virtual smorgasbord—the key is to put some forethought into what you want before placing your order. Casey, a 48-year-old man, had a good point: "'Time is Money' is no longer valid. Time is far more valuable than money." Time is the one resource that we have available to us as individuals that cannot be replenished. How we spend our time is how we are spending our lives. Casey continued, "Correct choice in a partner demands time and investigation." If you seriously want to find a life partner, you need to put some time into the process, but it is wise to spend your time well.

On one hand, Internet dating saves time and money, because you don't have to hang out in bars or nightclubs waiting to meet just one person. In the same amount of time on the Net, you can talk with many people. On the other hand, time can be swallowed up online in such a manner that hours fly by like minutes. People get into chat rooms and find themselves typing away for 6 hours at a time. I had a friend who realized she was reading profiles and chatting online for as many as 35 hours a week! While online dating requires time and effort, being clear about who you are, what you want, and what you have to offer—which this book will help you do—can save you tremendous amounts of time. Your honesty online can save other people huge amounts of time as well. As you read through *Virtual Foreplay*, consider your strategy. Time spent on preparation and asking yourself the pertinent questions posed here will certainly focus your efforts toward a more successful—and efficient—experience with online dating.

We were all raised on fairy tales in which the prince and princess magically came upon each other in the forest, which of course is fairly rare—but there is something to be gained by looking at the story of Cinderella. The prince had to canvas the whole town looking for the woman who fit his criterion, the glass slipper. He didn't try the shoe on only the beautiful, thin, and elite women; he tried it on everybody. The prince did, however, have a clear criterion and a strategy for accomplishing his goal. Would he ever have thought that Cinderella, the cleaning girl who had no money and a totally dysfunctional family, would be his ultimate match? I say this with tongue in cheek, but sometimes we have to put in some effort, look beyond our usual stomping grounds and beyond our "type," to find our perfect match. The Internet makes this easy.

One Christian dating site addressed the issue of time and effort in a particularly humorous way. At the bottom of its enrollment page it said that their organization "discourages you from joining if you are in a rush or are not seeking a long-term commitment, as you can not expect to find a spouse on Friday, go out on Saturday, and get married on Sunday." A good point, don't you think?

2

Twenty-first-Century RelationSHOP

W HEN THE GOING GETS TOUGH, the tough go shopping! The Internet has brought us the ease of shopping for absolutely anything from the convenience of our homes, and now we can even go "relationshopping!" On the Web, like nowhere else, we are able to try a relationship on for size and quickly leave it behind if it doesn't fit. You can try on long-distance relationships, exclusively online relationships, or face-to-face encounters. Our chat rooms have become metaphorical dressing rooms—or undressing rooms, for some! Knowing what you are "shopping for" will greatly enhance your online dating success.

There are many different perceptions about what online dating actually is and many different options for participating in it. For some, online dating means that you make contact with someone online and keep the entire relationship online, with no intention of ever meeting. To others, the Internet is just a tool for making initial contact, with the intention of meeting in person as soon as possible and carrying on from there. Others have met in person, established a basic attraction, and then used e-mail and the phone to get to know each other better before taking the next step.

One man, Larry, told me that this was the case in his relationship. He had met his girlfriend at a class on the West Coast, but she lived on the East Coast. They had established a definite interest in person but spent the next year or so online, sending each other e-mails. Larry explained, "It was very romantic. We shared so much with each other before we spent more time in person. We developed our connection on a really deep level, building a strong foundation, before we moved into the day-to-day realities of being together."

There are also those who use the Internet for meeting or enhancing their sexual desires and fantasies. This activity also seems to have a wide range of variations, from cyber voyeurism—looking at pictures and reading stories, much as one would read *Playboy* or *Penthouse*—to cyber sex—exchanging sexually explicit e-mail or, much like phone sex, engaging in sexually oriented live chats with another person. Webcams—cameras that can be mounted on top of a computer—are the latest way to peek into someone's bedroom while chatting online. All this gives new meaning to the term "touch typing"!

The reasons for online dating are just as varied as the ways to participate. Most of the people online have a sincere interest in finding a partner, or at minimum are looking for friends and pen pals. There are also quite a few married people who are seeking a diversion from a lonely or monotonous marriage, or searching for actual affairs or cyber flings. Often, what starts out as an attempt for contact and communication transforms into a fantasy that gets taken to the next step. Story after story has been passed around about "Mrs. So-and-So" who left "Mr. So-and-So" for the guy who was her online pen pal. While some of the rules for dating are different online, many of the common sense ones, like "don't carry on with a married person," still apply. The outcome of breaking such rules is rarely happy. While there is no right or wrong approach to virtual dating, there are definite consequences associated with different actions.

While I said that *Virtual Foreplay* isn't strictly a book of do's and dont's, you will find in it requests from the people you will be interacting with online, the first of which is for clarity and honesty:

▦ **If you are going to date online, decide what your goal is and be up-front about it.**

If you are not up-front about your reason for being online and your availability, it is false advertising. The implicit underlying message of posting a profile is, "I'm interested in and ready for a relationship." When that isn't really the case, it can be frustrating and hurtful. Todd, 45, complained, "I started talking with one woman online and we spent several months sending really great letters back and forth. At some point, I suggested we take the next step and start talking on the phone. She declined, saying that she wanted to 'take it slow.' If several months of writing before even talking on the phone isn't slow, then I don't know what is!" He went on to say that it seems like some people are just looking for a pen pal and aren't serious about getting into a real relationship. "It's not that I wouldn't have written to her anyhow, as online friends, it's just that I would have known what to expect and wouldn't have been so disappointed." Of course, my advice as an advocate of intellectual foreplay is that Todd should also get into the habit of asking early on what his e-date's intentions and time lines are. Establishing this in the beginning could have saved him a lot of anguish. By the same token, had she been clear up front without having to be asked, the whole situation could have been avoided.

In order to be clear with *other people* about your intentions in being online, you must first be clear with yourself about your reasons, as well as your readiness.

- **What kind of relationship are you really "shopping" for?**

- **Is the timing right in your life for you to begin e-dating now? Are you available—physically and emotionally?**

- **If you end up meeting someone online who intrigues you, would you be willing to meet them in person? How soon? Under what circumstances?**

One woman in her 60s, Nancy, shared her dismay. "I met this wonderful man on the Internet. At first we just exchanged e-mails back and forth, and I looked forward to opening my e-mail box each day. After a few weeks, we progressed to real-time instant messages. It then progressed to private and intimate chats, at which point I was really starting to fall for him and he for me, and we began talking about meeting in person. He then enthusiastically shared that in a few months he was taking a sabbatical from his position to spend a year teaching overseas. I wanted to share his excitement but all I could think, and eventually ask, was, 'why did you post your profile online and start a relationship, right before you were leaving for a year?' Apparently, he hadn't been thinking about the long-term implications of actually meeting someone online with whom he might want to continue a relationship. He apologized for the lack of forethought. We are still writing, now halfway across the world, but a year is a long time, so I'm not holding my breath." She added, smiling hopefully, "You never know, though!" Again, remembering to ask about the other's intentions, as well as your own, is always a wise step.

Long-Distance Romance

Our planet continues to get smaller and smaller. With our abilities to travel the globe physically and communicate electronically in an instant, people are making friends, doing business, and finding mates all around the world. Thus, more and more people are having to determine whether they are willing to engage in a long-distance romance and how to negotiate the challenges and benefits that it can bring.

Cheryl wrote to tell me about Dan, whom she met online. He lived in Hong Kong, while she lived in the United States. One positive aspect of the whole thing was that they ended up meeting at places in between, which allowed them to enjoy time together in Hawaii and Bali. While meeting in beautiful places and vacationing together is great, it is also not the most realistic setting for determining your day-to-day compatibility. One of the obvious challenges of a long-distance relationship is that if you ever want to be together on a regular basis, one of you is going to have to move. It is one thing to move from one town to another, or even from one state to another, but moving from one country to another creates a lot of instant challenges to overcome.

As I look back on my history of dating, prior to and including meeting Steve, I have to admit that several geographic moves I made were either toward or away from relationships. The excellent part of this is that, regardless of the long-term success of the relationship, I ended up living in some really wonderful places—Santa Barbara, Kauai, Carmel, Maui—and being exposed to different lifestyles, activities, and people. The difficult part was that every time I up and moved for a relationship, it totally disrupted my career and my support system of friends and family. The moves expanded and enhanced those very things, in different ways, as well.

In a world of busyness, long-distance relationships can have several benefits. One of these is that when you have a designated time to get together, the rest of your life is your own time. Jeff explained, "I like having a long-distance relationship because I don't have to be available 24/7 for someone else. This way, I work, go to the gym, have time with my other friends, and see my girlfriend on the weekends. I know it sounds sort of compartmentalized, but for me it just works better than always having to worry about whether she is expecting to get together every day."

When Steve and I were dating long distance, after several months it became obvious that, if we wanted this relationship to work, we needed to be in the same place fairly soon. Too many other people and opportunities were knocking on both our doors. Sara shared a similar experience. "I've always heard that 'absence makes the heart grow fonder,' but I've also heard, 'out of sight, out of mind.' I've been doing the long-distance relationship thing for almost a year, and at this point, we need to make a decision and either be together or just be friends." If you are not willing to participate in a long-distance relationship, be very thoughtful before you respond to the profiles or e-mails of people who live outside your area.

▣ **To what extent is geography an issue to you?**

▣ **Are you willing to move for a relationship?**

▣ **What would be the costs and benefits?**

▣ **How do you feel about long-distance relationships?**

A Wide Span of Ages on the Net

A particularly exciting aspect of the online dating community is the ever-growing group of seniors on the Net. While once we didn't think of the singles "industry" as including the 60-and-over crowd, there are now chat rooms and dating sites dedicated to seniors, as well as senior search options on the standard dating sites. Regardless of whether they choose to meet in person or not, online dating is providing a way for seniors to simply interact with other people, rather than feel alone. Jean, a woman in her 60s, said, "If I get lonely, I just jump on the Internet! I get to converse with many people of varied backgrounds." At a time of life when many people are faced with isolation and the loss of friends, online dating provides a convenient and easy way to make new friends and meet new sweethearts.

Unfortunately, age is one of the things people are compelled to lie about on the Net. A gay man told me that he put his age as 49 in his profile, even though he was 50, because he felt 50 was the magic number that would severely decrease the number of responses he would receive. Several women complained that men their age, 55 and up, were looking for women much younger than themselves.

Age discrimination appears to be practiced not only between the generations, but also within them.

Having access to a wide range of experience and wisdom via the Net can be a wonderful opportunity. There is a great story about two deer, an old buck and a young fawn, who are on opposite sides of a meadow. The fawn looks up and sees the old buck and thinks, "Wow, look at that buck, how wise he must be! Look at those antlers! Think of all the experience he has had and how much I could learn from him—but what would he want to talk to an inexperienced deer like me for?" The old buck looks up, sees the fawn, and thinks, "Oh look at that young deer, so innocent and full of life. How I would love to talk with her and see the world through her fresh eyes—but what would she want to talk with an old buck like me for?" They both turn and walk away, feeling unworthy of the other's attention.

▧ **Reach out and touch someone on the Net!**

▧ **What is the age range of people you are interested in meeting?**

▧ **What are your preconceptions about people in different age groups, and how do they limit your ability to find a potential mate or new friends?**

▧ **Are you comfortable with your own age, or do you feel compelled to lie about how old/young you are?**

Compassion Online

Ordinarily, we all buy into the philosophy—in theory if not in practice—that "honesty is the best policy." However, perhaps there are exceptions for which we need to have compassion. The tricky thing about being honest about who you are and what you are looking for on the Net is that, in some cases, the truth just isn't attractive. We live in a judgmental society that is often quite shallow and quick to dismiss anyone who doesn't fit a certain mold. While the majority of people on the Net are typical people who, for whatever reasons, are too busy to find someone in their daily lives, there are also people who consider themselves too shy, too unattractive, too fearful, or too different to attract attention if they reveal themselves.

There are also people on the Net who are terminally ill, seriously disabled, or incapable of performing sexually. These folks often feel that it isn't feasible or possible for them to get involved with someone physically when they aren't going to be able to participate in a "normal" relationship. It is desperately sad to see isolated or alienated people who are unable to receive attention or love because of a major setback that life has dealt them. For these people, the Internet has become a godsend, providing an anonymity that allows them to reach out and be received, and, for some, to put their disability aside for the first time in their life. Through role-playing they can be anyone they want to be—dashing, charming, and fully capable of interacting with others.

David found out that he had terminal lung cancer and was therefore unwilling to continue dating in the physical world. In his last 6 months, he began dating online, and since no one was aware of his terminal condition, and because of his obvious charm, he made many virtual conquests before he became physically unable to get online to participate. He said it was fantastic to be able to talk to people on a level completely removed from his physical condition—and painful to have to turn down the online playmates who were anxious to meet him in person.

From a place of compassion, it is easy to see why some people might be unwilling to post a profile that tells the whole truth about their situation. From that same place of compassion, we can even be joyful that technology has opened up a way for virtually everyone to have access to connection with other people. However, it would certainly be refreshing if someone were to simply say, "I don't want to meet in person; I just want to play online," or, "I have a terminal illness in my body, but plenty of love in my heart. Looking for an online playmate to soothe my final days. Willing to play? Guaranteed fun." My guess is that there are enough of us on the planet who would be willing to reach out and communicate, engage in cyber intimacy, and pray for the other's well-being.

> ▣ **How compassionate are you with other people's challenges and differences—online and off? Do you reach out to others? What do you allow to get in the way of being someone's friend?**

> ▣ **How truthful are you about your own challenges and realities? Do you give people a chance to accept you as you are and show you compassion?**

Choosing a Site

In addition to choosing the kind of relationship you are looking for online, you need to choose the site or sites that you want to join as a member. This can be as daunting a task as deciding which person to contact from the millions of profiles listed. There are literally thousands of dating sites on the Web. If you haven't already browsed through some of them, you really should poke around a bit; many let you do this free as a visitor. While most sites offer similar features, there are some significant differences.

When you are choosing a site, it is a good idea to have a clear picture of your own values and make your decision based on them. If you don't want sexually oriented responses, pick a site that doesn't allow "adult" or pornographic content. Most of the sites are specific about what they will and won't allow. While there are free sites as well as those with fees, the pricing varies from site to site, as does the length of the trial membership. My research has shown that most of the free sites attract a more sexually oriented group of people, while the sites with a paid membership attract people who are more serious about finding a lasting relationship.

Not only do sites vary in terms of cost and how many members they have, but some cater to specific audiences. Some specialize in certain age, religious, or ethnic groups; others are based on professional alliances, athletic interests, geographic areas, or sexual orientation. There are even dating services for prison inmates online! As you consider what your own special interests are, you can search out sites that will be full of like-minded individuals.

The major online dating sites have a general membership that spans the globe and includes every personality type. They assist you in making a match not by limiting membership but rather by providing search features that filter profiles based on your personal specifications. These search features serve as an electronic matchmaker for you.

Since it is not possible to list all the different sites here, my listing will refer you to some of the biggest ones, as well as some online directories that list hundreds of the smaller sites available. If your religious affiliation is important to you, note that there are sites dedicated specifically to helping people of a certain faith find each other. JDate.com offers a large membership for professional Jewish singles, while ChristianSingles.com, CatholicSingles.com, and SinglesWithScruples.com are a few of the many Christian sites. The online directories listed below will make it easy to find sites that match your own affiliations. Joining more than one site at a time is quite a common practice, although this becomes a time management problem quickly if you're not careful. The following descriptions were submitted by the sites themselves in order to assist you in sorting out the differences between them.

While this list was accurate at the time of printing, these companies change hands with some regularity, upgrade and add features constantly, and increase membership steadily! Use this as a guide to do your own research, recognizing that things change quickly!

Major Online Dating Sites

AmericanSingles.com

If you're trying to find that special person who is "one in a million," AmericanSingles.com is the place to look. With approximately three million registered members, AmericanSingles.com, one of the Internet's oldest and most recognized dating brands, provides its members with a safe, clean, and comfortable online environment for meeting and interacting with other singles. Members also enjoy AmericanSingles.com's other first-rate features, including free registration, complete privacy, relationship and dating experts, a twice-monthly newsletter, and an in-house travel department that organizes excursions for singles to locations around the world.

Date.com

Date.com has more than 200,000 members all across the globe. It offers a free trial membership to access the database with a small monthly fee for contacting the members. Date.com provides an advanced technology that makes the site fast and easy to use. The site also offers chat rooms, virtual gifts, a world-class dining guide, horoscopes, articles, and message boards.

DATINGfaces.com

DATINGfaces offers a personal page that members can easily customize to reflect their own characteristics and preferences. With half a million members and thousands joining weekly, DATINGfaces provides photos, profiles, and personalities of some of the most engaging singles on the Internet. Features like private one-on-one chats, meaningful Compatibility Smartz™ rankings, and a finely tuned astrological guide are offered. Members are provided with quick sign-ups, individualized searches, and a fun and positive online experience.

Friendfinder.com

FriendFinder.com is a leader in online dating personals for a good reason. It has over nine million registered members, making it very easy to find people that fit with everything you're looking for. From physical features to hobbies to location, it's fun to search for someone special to connect with. The Friend Finder site also has an instant messaging feature and chat rooms that are always busy with members meeting and getting to know each other. You can even exchange love/dating advice in the Relationship Magazine, join a Relationship Workshop, and check out your daily horoscope. Friend Finder is free to join, but paid membership upgrades are available and offer some added perks such as ensuring that you stand out on the top of search results.

Kiss.com

Kiss.com provides a fun, safe site offering content and services for singles seeking meaningful romantic relationships. With over 2.2 million registered members, Kiss.com is one of the world's top sites, providing an easy and convenient way for singles to discover love and romance from around the corner to around the world. In addition to an enormous database of qualified active singles, Kiss.com features Romance Wizard™ (an advance search system), Anonymous KissMail, Kiss Chats with featured guests, offline events through the US and abroad, travel opportunities, and advice.

LoveCity.com

Lovecity.com has about 175,000 members and boasts an almost equal ratio of male (55 percent) to female (45 percent) members—unlike many other sites, which have a higher ratio of men to women. LoveCity.com offers two types of memberships: free and upgraded. Free memberships allow users to place an ad at no cost, but they can respond only to members who contact them first. Upgraded memberships offer users the ability to contact as many members as they like.

Match.com

Match.com offers one of the largest databases of singles on the Web—more than five million registrations have been recorded to date, and there are currently one and a half million profiles available for searching. Match.com is geared toward singles seeking serious relationships, so each profile is screened to keep the site PG rated and focused on finding matches, not one-night stands or discreet affairs. Anonymous e-mail allows members to communicate indefinitely without sharing personal information. Two-way matching provides a listing of members who meet the searcher's criteria and who are also likely to be interested in someone like them—compatibility is ranked by percentage. The site is mostly free; there is no charge for posting a profile or photo or replying to any member. To initiate contact with another member, however, a paid membership is required.

Matchmaker.com

Matchmaker is a leading online community for meeting and socializing with new people. It has one of the largest databases of users on the Internet, with more than five million registered members and over one hundred metropolitan, lifestyle, and religious sites. Matchmaker was created more than 15 years ago and started as a message board service. More than 50,000 new members join each week; 200,000 per month. Matchmaker.com serves more than seventy-five local metropolitan areas across the United States, six other countries, and sixteen lifestyle communities. Members can find other members through location, religion, lifestyle, or a combination of all three.

People2People.com

People2People.com is an online singles community with over one million members worldwide. Two-way matching provides members with a listing of other members with whom they are most compatible. The site also features recorded voice greetings and video greetings, a "featured members" photo gallery, and a mall that allows members to send gifts to other members using only a screen name.

Membership subscriptions vary, with something to fit everyone's budget.

SocialNet.com

With no global barriers, SocialNet.com provides access to one of the Internet's largest database of singles in the world with over three million members and 8,000 new members daily. The site provides its members with an efficient way to meet others within a particular area code, region, or far away exotic location. SocialNet.com members create a custom profile that has more than 250 questions about their education, occupation, income level, hobbies, sports, and other interests. Members receive step-by-step instructions and many additional features to make online dating fun, safe, and fulfilling.

Udate.com

Udate operates a high-quality online singles community that stresses service, efficiency, and personal security. Its vaunted technology enables members to identify, communicate with, and meet people with whom they are psychologically, culturally, educationally, and demographically compatible. The company's state-of-the-art database, website design, and matchmaking features separate it from the competition. Individually customized page views provide members with the capability to meet compatible and interesting new friends in a fun and effective way.

Online Dating Directories

Aarens.com

Cupidnet.com

Internetdating.net

SingleSites.com

SinglesStop.com

Most people don't make a conscious decision about which site they want to join. Usually what happens—and what the sites hope will happen—is that the users log on as free guests to look around, see how the site works, and check out the people online. They often see several people who interest them, but are unable to talk to members—or are limited in doing so—until they become paid members as well. Hence, the choice to join a service doesn't necessarily have as much to do with the site itself, but rather with the members a person is interested in contacting.

Seven Steps to Dating Online

Here are some quick notes for those of you who want to try online dating (the first of which should really be "Finish reading this book!")

1 **Pick a reputable, well-known site that has a large user base.** The more people that are logged on as users, the more options you will have to choose from! Choosing a site with values similar to your own is always a good idea. If you don't want to receive pornographic messages, choose a site that doesn't have "adult" content. If you are taking this dating process seriously, look for a site that asks deep questions in its questionnaire and offers essay questions that yield important and interesting information.

2 **Fill out the registration questionnaire seriously and honestly.** Be truthful! The more you know who you are, what you want, and what you have to offer, the more likely you are to recognize a good match and the more likely the match is to recognize you. The exercises in *Intellectual Foreplay* and *Virtual Foreplay* are excellent for clarifying your interests and values, which you will want to weave into your personal profile.

3 **Practice intellectual foreplay online.** Ask and answer questions! Pay attention to the answers! The more you ask, the more

information you will have. Identify your nonnegotiable issues as a starting point for discussion. Keep your own values and ideals in mind as you explore with a potential partner. *Intellectual Foreplay* will provide you with many questions to help you get to know your online "date" better.

4 Take the communication to the phone. Tone of voice can tell you a lot. When we are restricted to reading e-mail, it is easy to read emphasis or meaning into the written word that isn't really there. When you talk on the phone, you will pick up subtle information that will either increase your interest or diminish it. You will also be able to tell more easily over the phone if someone has been drinking, if they call obsessively, or if they are polite. Good communication requires listening and speaking skills, which cannot be determined through e-mail alone.

5 Practice safe dating. We've all heard a lot about practicing safe sex, but it is equally important to practice safe dating. When you meet someone online, be careful not to give them information that will lead them to you physically until you are sure that they are a safe and trustworthy person. Unlike a blind date, in which you have the benefit of a personal referral, with an Internet introduction you don't really know to whom you are talking. Even the picture they send you could be of someone else. Practice due diligence, even if it means checking references before you agree to meet in person.

6 Trust your intuition. If something doesn't quite feel right or safe, *trust that feeling.* Our bodies often give us signs of discomfort when we are in any kind of danger. Does your head begin to ache? Does your stomach feel tight? Are you fidgeting? Pay attention to your body's signals.

7 **When the time comes to meet, do so in a neutral zone.** So you've been sending e-mails back and forth and are pretty sure that something beautiful could develop. Where and how do you meet— in his domain or hers? Neither! Meet in a neutral zone where you are both on equal footing and responsible for your own transportation. I offer relationship workshops on Maui for just that purpose. Meet in a safe, fun, supportive, and educational environment to discover whether or not you are a match.

3

The Rules Have Changed

MARY, A 45-YEAR-OLD WOMAN, just went through a divorce after 25 years of marriage to a man she had dated in high school. Suddenly she found herself in the singles world and had no clue what to do. "I found that after all those years, the rules had changed! Women no longer have to wait for men to call; in fact, we even dance with each other now instead of waiting for the guys to ask!" A friend referred her to the Internet as a great way to meet men without having to know or follow a certain set of rules.

Many of the norms that applied to dating behavior over the years do not apply online or at least are not being followed. Granted, some of them no longer apply offline either—or have exceptions—but for many of us they are deeply ingrained as the correct way to do things. They crop up as part of our underlying belief system whether we rationally believe in them or not. This chapter will guide you to look at a few of your underlying beliefs and analyze whether they are still serving you. If not, this is your chance to create new guidelines for effective dating in the 21st century.

If you find certain attitudes *are* a part of your belief system, it will help to be aware of and explicit about them, to avoid confusing the people with whom you are interacting online. A gentleman by the name of Lou offered a great point: "My idea of rules for dating is to find out what the other person's rules are and to respect them."

Thanks for the Date. What's Your Name?

One man I was interviewing for this book wrote in an online instant message, "An odd thought just struck me. You are the only woman I've ever chatted with online using real names. In the words of Jerry Seinfeld, "What's up with that?" Times have definitely changed! Where once the first thing you asked if you were interested in someone was their name, now you only get a username. In the old days, if there was definite interest, the second thing you would ask for was the person's phone number. Now both name and phone number are privileged information and are not given out haphazardly.

Dating is a bit backwards online: where once we would meet, exchange names and phone numbers, and then reveal personal information about ourselves on a date, now we find out all kinds of personal information first, then we meet, and then, maybe, give out our names and our phone numbers.

Talking to Strangers

Remember when you were little and your parents told you not to talk to strangers? We still pass those words of wisdom on to our children, but there are an awful lot of exceptions! On the Internet, as in our daily lives, we connect with strangers on a daily basis. If we followed the old rule while dating online, we would never meet anyone. What has been a tried-and-true rule throughout time has to be stretched in order for us to reach out on the Web.

The "don't talk to strangers" rule was designed to keep us from getting into unsafe situations with people we don't know well enough to trust. Now we are finding that it isn't so much the act of "talking" with strangers that merits concern, but rather what we say, how much we divulge, whether we trust our intuition, and whether we choose safe places and times to meet.

▨ **When is a stranger no longer a stranger? Does sharing e-mail full of personal details turn the person into a friend? Does talking on the phone?**

▨ **Is trust the criterion that turns someone into a friend? Can you trust someone you've never met?**

Knowing when you can trust someone is a hard thing to assess and is quite often based more on our intuition than on the answer to any of these questions. As Donna, a woman in her 30s, insightfully noted, "I've learned to trust my intuition; if he *seems* like a jerk he probably *is* a jerk!" On the other hand, I've exchanged e-mail with people online who were interested in my classes or books and, after sending a few letters back and forth, have felt as if they were friends whom I would feel very comfortable meeting. I've had to actually resist my trusting nature and follow the common-sense rules of not putting myself into a vulnerable position. With the Internet, the new "rule" seems to be: "Feel free to talk to strangers, but think twice before trusting them!"

▨ **How do you feel about talking to strangers?**

▨ **Do you handle this differently online than off?**

One woman in her early 30s offered this advice, "Always talk to strangers! You have no idea the positive impact you could have on not only their lives, but everyone they come into contact with, as well." It seems she made a point of brightening a stranger's day, spreading a little light via the Internet. That is certainly a nice approach! Perhaps if we did that offline as well, the lonely planet wouldn't be so lonely!

Women on the Move

One gentleman, Rick, was explaining to me the frustration that he was experiencing with women online due to the ingrained belief that women shouldn't make the first move. This was conflicting with the common "rule" of online dating that says women should not give out their phone number until they are sure about the other person. Rick explained, "Often, I meet women online, we exchange e-mails for a while and maybe participate in a chat or two, and then we start talking about meeting in person. Since I know women are cautioned not to give out their phone number, I give them mine and ask that they call to begin talking in "person" or to set up a meeting time and place. They will express a readiness or willingness in e-mail, but then I never hear from them. I think they are uncomfortable being the one to call; they don't want to be the pursuer."

Even in the 21st century, women and men are still a little confused over who should do what. The roles have changed and the guidelines have become fuzzy. Therefore, it is necessary for us to examine our own comfort zones and beliefs and be explicit about them. If you are unwilling to make the first move or make the phone call, say so, or at least don't indicate that you will. Men are just as confused as women on these issues, and a little clarity on both sides would be tremendously helpful.

Todd explained that he felt women expected men to contact them based on their profiles, but few women would contact the men. Lisa agreed, "I never contact a guy unless he contacts me first." Sally, a woman in her late 30s said, "As I browsed the profiles, I asked myself how I felt about initiating contact before I sent any e-mail, but it is now the 2000s and women are allowed to make the first move, even expected to. I realized I felt in power in the situation for once!"

Several other people said that they enjoyed the freedom of not having to play games or worry about what the other person would think if they made the initial contact. Jessica shared, "It is nice to be in an environment where I'm not expected to play hard to get. Why would I bother putting my profile up, saying 'I'm looking for my mate,' if my intention was to play hard to get?!" Carol said, "I have always been taught to go after what I want. So I completely ignore the 'women shouldn't...' anything rules." I can guarantee that Steve and I would never have met if I hadn't taken the initiative to go up and introduce myself. Not everyone has the same level of comfort, however, so you have to ask yourself some questions first. Explore your personal beliefs to be sure that you are working *with* them, rather than *against* them.

> ■ **How do you feel about women taking initiative to meet a man? As a woman, are you comfortable making the first move? As a man, how do you feel receiving the first contact?**

Once you achieve clarity about what you are and are not willing to do, a whole host of options for handling the challenges will reveal themselves. For instance, Sue compromised by giving out her voice mail number. While she was still responsible for taking the next step, *returning* a phone call didn't feel like the first move. This also let her hear his voice before she decided to call and allowed her the safety factor of being in control of who had access to her home number. She explained, "It still made a few guys really mad that I didn't give out my home number. A couple of them actually got pretty nasty about it, but if they can't empathize with the fact that I am a single mom fully responsible for my own safety and that of my son, then they are not the guys that I want to date."

Different people are comfortable connecting in different ways. The bottom line is that we each need to take a look at our belief systems and individual situations, take responsibility for what is comfortable for us, and honor what is comfortable to others. Why not just be explicit about what you are comfortable with in your profile or e-mail and see what happens?

Equal Billing

After Bob had had several dinner dates with women he'd met online, and never saw them again, he shared his suspicion that there are many women who are meeting guy after guy online strictly for free meals. While there is no way to assess whether the women that Bob met were trying to get a free meal or just decided not to go out with Bob again, it does bring up a hot topic for discussion, with a lot of differing opinions.

The expectation that men should pay the bill has become an area of tremendous confusion—and in some cases, resentment—for people dating, whether online or off. When women weren't working outside of the home, and thus didn't have the same access to money, this custom made a lot more sense than it does today. Regardless of your feelings about this—and the emotions certainly do range widely—the key is to first identify *what you believe* and *be very clear* about it.

When I shared this viewpoint with a group of single men and women, a couple of people got upset and asked, "How can you be clear about that tactfully?" With sarcasm they added, "Am I paying for this or are you?" Appreciating their confusion, I explained how I always addressed the issue, and offered a helpful way to communicate, on both sides, to minimize the problem.

When the bill came to the table on a date, I always simply asked casually, "Can I split that with you?" or "Can I contribute to the cause?" or reached for my wallet. If he wished to pay the bill, he could then simply say, "Thanks, but it's my treat." If he didn't want to pay for the meal, he could comfortably say, "Thanks. Your half is..." or "Why don't you get the tip and I'll cover the bill," or whatever suited him. There have been a few men who declined my offer, looking at me like I was being some kind of independent feminist, but I'd rather offend someone by being independent than have them think I was using or taking advantage of them. This is just my style and makes for clear communication with few misunderstandings. Most men went ahead and paid in spite of my offering, which, of course, I appreciated. However, if I were absolutely not interested in someone at all, I would not allow him to pay for me, as I would not want to lead him on. When a woman insists on paying her own way, it generally sends a very clear message that you are simply friends, or that it is too soon to tell whether you will be anything more.

On the other hand, it would clear up a lot of confusion for a woman if a man would simply say, when asking the woman out, "Can I treat you to dinner?" or "Would you like to go to the concert? *My treat.*" This clearly states that he is paying. Sometimes, this is automatically understood. "Let me take you to a really nice place" implies that he is expecting to pay. "Do you want to meet me somewhere for dinner?" is a little more vague. When meeting someone from the Net, it would be especially simple and reasonable to say, "Let's meet for lunch as friends, Dutch treat, and see what develops."

Expecting someone whom you have never met to pay your way regardless of whether or not you ever intend to see them again is not respectful. It would be much easier if everyone in the Internet dating scene were to pay their own way—or at least offer to—until they have established the nature of their interest. Whatever your preference, beliefs, or style, being clear up front can avoid a lot of discomfort and resentment.

> ▦ **What are your feelings about when it is appropriate or expected for a man to pay? How do you feel about a woman offering to pay or insisting on paying?**

Honesty Is the Best Policy

The rule that is broken most often on the Net is the age-old wisdom that we should tell the truth. On the Internet, people tend to be more honest in their reactions to others—often painfully so—and more disclosing of their personal life stories and experiences. Where they tend to be more dishonest is in their assessment of themselves or in putting up out-of-date or glamorous photos that do not accurately represent their true looks. Sometimes this dishonesty is simply a lack of self-awareness. People often do not see themselves accurately and therefore say what they *think* is true, but doesn't appear to be true to anyone else.

Leslie shared in her profile that she was fun to be with and had a good sense of humor. However, others perceived her as fairly serious. Frank had been athletic through his 20s and 30s and thus perceived himself to be fit and active. In his 40s, he had put on 20 pounds and watched more sports on television than he actually participated in; however, his self-image had not changed to match reality. His description of himself as athletic in his profile created a picture in the mind of the reader that didn't match his current physical state.

People also often say what they *wish were true* about themselves rather than what currently is true, or they paint a picture slightly more rosy than the reality. Joe, who was unemployed and sleeping on the beach, said in his profile, "I have learned that money doesn't bring happiness. I am embracing simplicity in my life." There is a certain attraction to a guy who understands the value of simplicity, but what is not clear here is that he has no money, no place to live, and no job.

Sometimes the dishonesty is an out-and-out attempt to deceive people. I've heard countless stories about people who put someone else's picture up with their profile; lie about their age—claiming to be younger or older; lie about their weight, their past, or their marital status. There are also people who are simply playing games: teenagers pretending to be adults, guys pretending to be women, and so on. As you read through profiles and e-mails, keep this very real possibility in mind before you lose your head over someone.

Sally told me: "I had been e-mailing a very polite, nice man. He told me he was 32 and lived in the same province as me. He persisted in asking for my telephone number to 'chat.' I am hesitant in divulging personal info, so each time he asked I told him I was enjoying the mystery. Well, one day when I logged on I had another e-mail from him—actually not really from him but *his mother!* She was reprimanding me; as it turned out her 13-year-old son had accessed the site and was playing out his every fantasy!" The "mystery" can easily turn out to be more than you bargained for.

If you are the one lying about an aspect of yourself, this is an area of your life at which you want to take a long, hard look. Aside from the game-playing, underneath the lie is often some form of shame or problem that seriously needs addressing if you want to have healthy relationships. You either need to work on changing your reality to make what you say about yourself true, or you need greater self-acceptance to become comfortable telling the truth. If someone is lying about their weight, it is because they do not feel satisfied with the truth and don't believe someone else will be satisfied with them either. If they lie about their age, they have issues with being too young or too old. If they lie about being married, they have an obvious problem with loyalty. Not only is the dishonesty itself a problem for a relationship, but the self-esteem issues underlying the lies will also sabotage a relationship. Self-esteem will be addressed more in Chapter 5: "Mirror, Mirror," and ways to tell if someone is lying to you will be discussed further in Chapter 8: "Practicing Intellectual Foreplay Online."

▨ **Take a careful, honest look at yourself. What are your best qualities? What is the evidence that your assessment is accurate?**

▨ **Are there aspects of yourself that you are uncomfortable telling the truth about? Are you willing to work on either changing your self-perception or changing your reality to better align the two?**

Funny enough, people can also be too hard on themselves. I've known many people who perceived themselves to be fat or ugly, when in fact they had perfectly beautiful features and healthy, normal bodies. Many of the people I interviewed about what online dating taught them shared things like, "I'm more datable than I thought I was," or "I'm more outgoing than I thought I was," or "I am more attractive than I thought I was." Since people's profiles are their own perceptions of themselves, the profile is often a better indicator of a person's self-concept than it is of the way the person appears to other people. The moral of the story is, take what you read with a grain of salt, and check it out for truthfulness as soon as you can— before you find yourself falling for a false image of another person.

No Means No!

Several women wrote to tell me that despite all the things they enjoyed about online dating, one of the most difficult issues was men who wouldn't take "no" for an answer. It seems that often a polite "Thanks, but no thanks" was either responded to with mean notes or ignored with a persistence that became not only annoying but sometimes frightening.

When I spoke with some of the men online about this issue, Dennis pointed out, "This is one of the areas that is challenging for men. In the physical world of dating, we are taught to be persistent and women are often taught to play hard to get. Women may say 'no' to our initial interest in them, but if we continue showering them with attention, they often eventually change their mind and give us a chance. We have learned that 'no' doesn't necessarily mean 'no' and a little further effort is worth our while. However, on the Internet, 'no' usually really means *'no'!* Since the woman has no more information about you than she had when she turned you down the first time, putting pressure on her with continued advances via e-mail generally only serves to scare her or make her angry, or both."

The moral of the story is that there are plenty of fish on the Net, as the old cliché now goes. If someone turns you down, respectfully move on. Rejection and projection will be discussed in Part IV, but for now suffice it to say that if a person has never met you, they can't really reject *you*. They may be reacting to something you said that reminded them of a past sweetheart, or they may be showing a fear of commitment because you sound too good to be true. You will never know, so you may as well count your blessings that you got out so easily, and move on.

- **What is your reaction when someone says "no" to you?**

- **How do you feel about saying "no" to other people? Are you able to do so respectfully or do you just ignore them?**

- **Are you different online than in person regarding this issue?**

Multiple Mailings

In the physical world of dating, we have some spoken and unspoken rules that if you are dating more than one person at a time, it is appropriate to let the other people know what, exactly, they are involved in—especially once emotions or sex are involved. In the world of e-mail interactions, however, "monogamy" doesn't seem to be the norm, although it's desired by many. As I polled online dating veterans, they repeatedly said that it is completely acceptable to cultivate multiple online friends, to send inquiries to several potential mates, and to "e-date" as many potentials as it takes to find the one with whom you want to develop a relationship. One woman explained, "I don't consider communication to be dating."

Where the online and offline worlds converge is around the issue of common courtesy in terms of telling the truth and being clear about your agreements. Once you indicate that there is any sort of exclusivity in your online relationship, you should honor that agreement by letting your other interests know.

Kendra wrote that she had an e-mail sent to her that said, "I love you and I want to marry you." When she looked at the e-mail more closely, she saw that her suitor had sent this exact same e-mail to 140 other women and hadn't bothered to blind copy them. All 140 address were visible to all! This is a definite breach of the unspoken online dating rules and isn't exactly what I mean about being up front about what you are doing!

Cindy admitted, "I am a flirt and have a tendency to attract and keep on attracting. I would actually prefer to be able to e-date only one person, but insecurities from my past tend to intrigue me into accumulating more and more 'virtual boyfriends.' I would never cheat on a man in real life, but I guess since sometimes I know that I'll never meet these guys, somewhere in the back of my mind I think that multiple e-dates are acceptable." She then admonished herself, "Doing as I do and accumulating too many people is totally unacceptable."

Whether online or off, the things to consider are your own values, how you would like to be treated, and, perhaps even more importantly, how your online partners would appreciate being treated. Cultivating multiple friends is one thing, but "collecting" virtual sweethearts and leading them all on could obviously be setting yourself, and your online paramours, up for a painful experience.

If you are just playing and don't expect to ever meet people in person, be explicit that you are strictly looking for an online relationship that stays in the cyber realm. There will undoubtedly be many people who are still willing to play with you at that level. In fairness to those who are seriously looking for a life mate, be upfront about your intentions—it's the honorable thing to do.

Are you, or are you willing to be, honest with your online partners?

⊞ **What are your beliefs about monogamy and at what stage in a relationship does it become important for you?**

Sex Before...Meeting?

I hate to make any commentary on former President Clinton, but he raised a question few of us could imagine in the physical world: "What actually counts as sex?" Most people recognize that there is a wide range of activities that "count" as sex, and oral sex—performed or received—is certainly one of them, but what about verbal sex? In the cyber world, the line becomes much fuzzier.

Certainly, we don't consider reading an adult magazine or watching a pornographic movie to be sex with the people in the pictures. Talking to a "professional" on a 900 number sex hotline is certainly a sexual encounter, but does it count as having sex with that person? What about having phone sex with someone you know or someone you might actually meet—does that nudge the line a little closer to being crossed?

On the Net, a whole new reality is taking place: interactive, real-time sexual encounters between real people who have never met, but could potentially meet. This technology has put temptation at our fingertips for anyone to access, from almost anywhere, at any time. I put out a survey online about whether people considered cyber sex—sexually explicit e-mails or interactive chats—to be sex. The answers volleyed back and forth: "No, it isn't," "Yes, it is."

⊞ **Does it count as sex if you never see or touch the other person?**

⊞ **Does it count if you are on real-time Webcams watching each other, but never meet?**

One woman commented, "Sex to me is physical intercourse. Everything else is foreplay." Another candidly stated, "It counts as sex if you only have one hand on the keyboard!" An 18-year old woman pointed out, "Cyber sex is like erotic fiction with feedback." While another woman exclaimed, "Cyber sex is my definition of safe sex. I am an education coordinator for our local hospital, and the programs I deal with are on sexually transmitted diseases. If people would only have cyber sex, then I wouldn't be needed at my job anymore!" She followed her comment with a joke about having job security!

The really tricky thing is that we don't all agree on whether cyber sex counts or not. Some say the emotions are the same; others say it is just fantasy and physical release, nothing more. Because everyone sees it differently, we have a responsibility—just like in our physical lives—to be explicit with the people with whom we are engaging in these activities. Ultimately, it doesn't really matter how it is defined to anyone other than yourself and the person you are doing it with, unless you are already in a real-life relationship. Then it also matters how your real-life partner feels.

I followed up the original survey question with an inquiry as to whether people would consider it cheating if they found that their partner was engaging in cyber sexual activities. I received the same mix of responses. The majority said that they would consider it disloyal, although less so than physically cheating. Almost everyone agreed, at the very least, that it would be a sign of a big problem in their relationship, especially if the activities were done in secrecy.

There is one other major reason why one should think about how cyber sex counts in the scheme of things, and that is the issue of sex before meeting! We have all entertained the question—and many have strong beliefs—about whether we think it is okay to have sex before marriage. Most of us, too, have entertained questions about whether it is okay to have sex on the first date or early in a relationship. But sex before meeting? Who would have ever thought!

It's not my place to make judgements about anyone's choice of activities, but rather I am here to help you look at the big picture as it pertains to you.

> ### If you really want to create a long-term or enduring relationship with someone you meet online, what kind of pressure will it put on your first meeting if you have already had sex online?

Sue told me that she had been e-mailing this guy back and forth for several exchanges before the e-mails started to get more suggestive. They ended up in a private chat one night and one word led to another until they were hot and heavy. Afterwards, there was a sense of discomfort because they'd shared something as personal as masturbation and a cyber orgasm with each other, but they hadn't even met. When they started to talk about actually meeting, she felt strange about it. Sue couldn't imagine standing face to face with a total stranger with whom she'd masturbated! On the other hand (if you'll pardon the pun), other people have said that the shell of intimacy they created online was easily filled with real intimacy when they actually met. They were able to step back, breathe a little, and slow things down until their physical beings caught up with their imaginations. The transition from virtual to physical will be addressed in greater detail in Part Five.

As mentioned earlier, there is a tendency when communicating online to think that what takes place in the virtual realm doesn't really count. However, judging by the countless number of people who are either heartbroken or feeling immense love due to the words that someone said to them online, it would appear that our interactions there definitely do count. Real emotions are evoked from words that seem to carry an even greater weight when put into print, and can be read and read again. To the receiver, they seem even more real than words that blow away on the wind.

☷ Do you make the same choices regarding sexual activity online as you do off? How would engaging in sexual exchanges online affect your ability to meet in person or affect an already existing relationship?

If you've been dating on the Net, then you already know this, but let me offer it again here as a reminder. Some of the people on the Net—as in the real world—are simply out to practice the art of seduction. Wendy, a 25-year-old, shared, "Online dating has been hard for me because all the guys want to do is 'cyber' and know how I am built." One guy in his early 20s, when asked how he'd benefited from online dating, said, "As crude as it might sound, I've found it's easy to find girls that are just in the mood for 'oral' sex online." Interestingly, when asked what he had learned about himself in the process of online dating, he shared, "that I don't enjoy the aftereffects of a one-night stand. I've also learned that intellectually it is just as easy for me to seduce women as it is for them to seduce me."

Remember that you really do not know the integrity of the person behind the words and there are some definite smooth talkers out there—men and women alike. A gay woman sent me her story: "I met a woman online who lived in LA and we immediately hit it off. We talked on the phone and I thought that she might be someone really special. She was funny, very romantic, and sexual. Well, by time I got to LA on a biz trip a few weeks later, she was in love with Ms. Miami online! Not only this, but she had women lining up out the door like a real stud! She was able to be very intimate over the Net yet she was unable to be intimate in real life. You have to be careful. Everyone can be wonderful until you find out that they are only sharing a part of themselves and are actually sitting in a jail cell e-mailing you!"

A man in his mid-30s said that what he likes best about online dating is "anticipating the first touch and knowing that if we manage to meet, she's mine—if I want. The thrill or challenge is eliminated if there's no chance of meeting. I'm well-mannered and attractive, combined with above-average eloquence and communication skills. I know ways to seduce, so things have been better for me than most. And it is quite discreet, too. No one really knows you, and improvising—sounds better than deceit?—can often be easy to accomplish." He then defined himself, "I'm attractive, devious, and a slut." My best guess is that this self-analysis is not in his profile, nor the first thing he shares with a potential partner. I'm sure she eventually figures it out, but it is helpful to be aware, in advance, that people like this are out there, waiting to "improvise" with whomever will let them.

Love and Marriage Before Meeting

One day, a 12-year-old girl, Liz, came into my office saying she was concerned that her girlfriend was going to blab a secret to other kids about Liz's mom getting married. My first reaction was that the problem was about her ability to trust her friend, but on second thought, I found it odd that her mom's wedding was a secret, so I asked why. Liz explained, matter-of-factly, "Oh, she doesn't want anyone to know she's getting married because she hasn't met him yet."

Inwardly surprised, I said calmly, "Tell me more about that." She went on to explain that a family friend had "introduced" her mom to this guy and their relationship of several months had taken place entirely via phone and e-mail. They had determined that they would meet the following month and if everything went smoothly, they would get married right away. I cringed at the potential for problems here, as I have counseled many adolescents and teens who hated their stepparents and were doing everything in their power to make their parents split up. Without wanting to plant any negative thoughts in Liz's head, I asked, "How do you feel about having a new stepfather that you have never met?" She simply smiled and said enthusiastically, "I think it's great."

Granted, there may have been something lost in the translation of a 12-year-old. Perhaps these two adults had been talking and writing to each other regularly and at some point explored what they ultimately wanted in a relationship. Determining that they were both hoping to get married, they agreed to meet and see if the relationship could move in that direction. Assuming that that was the scenario, rather than a totally whimsical engagement, what bothers me more is the girl's attitude that it is totally feasible to plan to marry someone that you have never met. While the trust in her mother's decision was admirable, I couldn't help wondering what life was going to be like for Liz as she grew up with the mind-set that the decision to get married, or introduce new parents to your children, is quite as simple as that. When we are parents, single or otherwise, we need to remember that everything we do is modeling for our children. Therefore, we must make wise choices and be sure that our children understand the whole range of thought processes and considerations that go into choosing a mate who may become a parent for our children.

Another girl, Toni, came into my office and confessed that she was totally in love with her boyfriend; however, she was worried that he may have been cheating on her. Feeling empathy for the confusion that dating can bring, especially at the age of 13, I was about to help her explore her feelings when her friend pitched in, "She's never met him, Ms. Hogan." My eyebrows undoubtedly went up as I turned back to look at Toni. She immediately started to explain that he was wonderful and that she'd never felt this way and that he loved her and she loved him, etc., etc. Apparently, this had been going on for several months and they had spent quite a bit of time on the Internet and the phone. There was no doubt in my mind that Toni was experiencing very intense feelings, but I had to wonder, was it love?

Some people may easily dismiss Toni's feelings because she is a teenager, but this experience is not unique to the young. It is reminiscent of situations in which people fall in love with inmates via the letters that they write or stories during war time of women writing to unknown soldiers, falling in love, and awaiting their return. Now, adults online are regularly claiming to have found the love of their lives in people they have never met. This phenomenon causes us all to question our beliefs about love.

🔲 **Can you truly love someone you have never met? Or, is the feeling the fantasy of love, or the desire for love?**

In the movie *You've Got Mail,* with Meg Ryan and Tom Hanks, there is a wonderful scene in which Meg Ryan's character, Cathleen, is breaking up with her boyfriend after discovering that neither of them is really in love with the other. Cathleen has been developing an online relationship with an unknown man, played by Hanks, and it has caused her to rethink her relationship with her boyfriend. As they are breaking up, her boyfriend asks her, "Is there someone else?" She looks hesitant for a moment, not sure how to respond, and then answers wistfully, "No, but there is the dream of someone else."

Online and In Love

We must examine our own feelings and emotions and be watchful of how we define and label them. The Internet is a great tool for meeting people, and having intimate, honest, and deep conversations is a very stimulating process. Our cyber friends fill our hearts with support and companionship. We feel listened to, cared for, honored, and all of that is grand. Those elements create a perfect environment where love can grow.

🔲 **Could true love for the other person evaporate if we were to meet them face-to-face?**

🔲 **Is it that the illusion we have created would then be shattered?**

The intensity of our feelings when we connect with people online, and sometimes offline as well, is based on the degree of our passion and our capacity for love. The other person is mirroring back to us our own love for ourselves, for life, for ideas—whatever the content is that we share. This feeling reveals to us our intense love for love, the foreplay to love with another person, but is it love *for* the other person? These are questions that you must ask and answer for yourself.

By contrast, when we go through a breakup with someone, even if we know that parting ways is the right thing to do, even if we're instigating the breakup, it is often devastating. When I was in graduate school, I broke up with a boyfriend of 4 years. I was heartbroken even though I knew breaking up was right. One of my college professors, Dr. George Brown, pointed out that what I was actually mourning *was the loss of what I had hoped the relationship would become,* more than the loss of the actual relationship. When I stopped crying long enough to digest what he was saying, I could see that he was right. *I was grieving the loss of the illusion* that this man would love me and want to marry me and be faithful to me and live happily ever after—none of which was the reality of the relationship at all.

Before you start thinking that I have no sense of romance, let me offer you another story. Nathan met a woman in a chat room who lived in another country. She invited him into a private chat room and they ended up talking for 6 straight hours about "everything and nothing." They then continued their friendship with instant chats and e-mails. He explained, "It got to where the only reason I went on the Net was to talk to her. My heart raced whenever she was online, kind of like a teenager falling in love for the first time. I then realized that I was in love with her and finally got up the nerve to tell her. Her response was that she had known for months and was just waiting for me to figure it out. She has been my best friend. She tells me the truth and has always told me what I needed to hear, not what she thought I wanted to hear, whether I liked it or not. Sometimes we'd end up mad at each other, but we have always been able to talk about it instead of the usual screaming, pouting, leaving the room, and ignoring each other that most people do. We talk on the phone now once a month and we are still best friends to this day. She loves me and I love her, but we both know that due to circumstances—she is married and lives on the other side of the globe—we will never be together. She will always have a very special place in my heart, forever and a day."

I was practically in tears by the time I finished his letter. It reminded me of the deliciously tragic love story *The Bridges of Madison County.* Who am I to say that Nathan and his lady friend, who have meant so much to each other and have supported each other so beautifully, are not really in love? At the same time, one can't help but wonder what is love *for the other person,* and what is love *for the fantasy* of who we think the other person is, or the tantalizing draw of forbidden or unrequited love. Without their ever having met, it is a virtual relationship—a relationship in essence, but not quite in fact.

> **If you want a real-life relationship, take your online relationship offline as soon as it is safe and possible. Give yourselves the test of reality before your imagination creates an image with which reality cannot compete.**

When I was 13, I fell in love with Bruce, a boatman I met while on a river trip vacation. (Egads! Are we seeing a pattern here?) We shared my first kiss and then began writing to each other regularly. Back in those days, personal computers and the Internet were not yet in existence, and phone calls were expensive; as teenagers, we certainly couldn't pay for them. We had the advantage of having met in person—and shared initial feelings for each other—but absence made the heart grow fonder. I remember, just as Nathan described, my heart racing at just the glimpse of Bruce's handwriting on the envelope.

The problem was that the longer that we were apart, the more I filled in the gap between us with my imagination, daydreaming about who he was and how things could be. I fantasized about running away to be with him and living happily ever after. I remember my mom explaining to me that I was experiencing the classic syndrome of a "phantom lover," but I didn't want to believe her. I wanted my vision to be real. Bruce really didn't stand a chance when we got together again a few years down the road, as wonderful as he truly was, because the custom-ordered fantasy of perfection in my yearning teenage heart posed some serious competition. Suddenly, the relationship was no longer the one-sided creation of my imagination; he had free will and could react to me and interact with me however he chose. (Gee—imagine that!)

Without the reality of having to pay bills, clean house, make dinner, deal with moods, compromise on time schedules, agree on television shows, negotiate the quality and quantity of sexual encounters, etc., it is easy to yearn for a relationship that we imagine is perfect. With online or long-distance relationships, not only do we not have these day-to-day realities to deal with, we also get to pick the time we want to engage with the other person. We can wait until we are rested or in the mood. If we don't want to interact, we can simply stay off the computer or wait to respond. Via e-mail, we also have the opportunity to think carefully about what we want to say and its potential impact, and to edit before we send. To a certain extent, the same is true in a chat. Even though it is interactive, the very act of typing our reply allows us a moment to think before we speak, which is a moment that can save us a lot of difficulties with another person.

In offline relationships, we can also experience this same sort of illusion. Many relationships are destroyed when we encounter someone we are attracted to, or have a passionate but short affair with, and then imagine is perfect or at least more desirable than the person we are already involved with. Without putting the relationship through the test of time and day-to-day reality, we simply don't have enough information to know whether what we imagine is true.

The Key to Your Heart

My philosophy is that all around us and within us is a never-ending source of love that we can access at any time. There doesn't have to be an object for our affection in order for us to feel love, as our souls are love. Our natural state is love. What happens to most of us, though, is that we close our hearts, which is like closing a door so that the love cannot stream in or out freely. The term "You hold the key to my heart" applies to the experience in which someone is able—through their words, touch, smile, or chemistry—to help us unlock the door. The love of our soul then floods us, filling our being. The person who helps us to open our heart becomes the object of that love, out of our gratefulness to them for helping us experience our soul's capacity.

Relationships can be such a beautiful flow of love between two open hearts. We help someone to feel the love within them; they help us to feel the love within us; and we share our love with each other. Our love runs over and spills onto everything around us. We become different. When we are in love with someone, we feel love for everything in our lives more easily. The access is open.

The sad thing is that we often credit the other person entirely for the way we feel, when we actually have had that capacity for love all along. The problem with giving them all the credit is that, if the person then leaves us, we think we no longer have the key, or the access to that source. Suddenly, we close the door to our heart and feel cut off from love entirely. So often we give our power away, thinking that someone else holds the only set of keys, leaving ourselves feeling empty or powerless without the other person.

However, we can open the door ourselves. We can love God, we can love life, we can love nature, we can love our selves, and we can love love. By raising our self-esteem, accessing the well of love within, we can live in alignment with our souls—*in love all the time.* By doing so, we will have much more love to share with others, and perhaps even more importantly, we will not cling to our mates like energy vampires, in search of love that they really can't give us. We have to feel love within. When two people come together who are already feeling love, for themselves and for life, they have more love to share and don't need the other person in order to feel complete. Being together simply amplifies the joy.

Here is the kicker. Is it possible to love someone who doesn't love you in return? Of course it is, and most of us have. *The other person's participation is not required for us to feel love.* The love is within us; it is who we are, and other people just help us access it. When we encounter someone online who we don't know and they say loving, kind, comforting, or romantic things to us, we begin to open the door to our hearts and let our love flow. *We must accept and rejoice in this feeling of love as our own, as the other person may not even be who they say they are.* It may be a man saying he is a woman. It may be a woman pretending to be a man. It may be a teenager pretending to be an adult. It could be a creep pretending to be an angel. Until we really know this person, we need to rejoice in having an open heart and acknowledge that feeling of love for what it is.

With online dating or personal ads, it is easy to feel love bubbling to the surface as we read about walking on the beach hand in hand together, but then feel nothing when we meet in person. Recognizing that it wasn't the other person that brought you those feelings of love, but that you actually just accessed your own source of love, can help you to recognize that the love didn't go away from you when that person was gone—you just closed the door again. The other person never held the key in the first place; they just activated your choice to love. This is important to recognize because it allows us to make life a treasure hunt for the multitude of keys that can open our hearts, helping us to be more loving and to feel more love throughout our lives, regardless of what the people around us choose to do.

🔲 **As you read profiles online or e-mails that people send you,
pay attention to which words, concepts, values, and activities
cause you to feel love. What causes you to feel hopeful? What
pulls at your heartstrings? By doing this, you will come to
know yourself better; you will begin the treasure hunt for
your very own set of keys to your heart. Start making a list of
those little keys.**

Code of Ethics

Making sense of the world when it keeps changing can be challenging. There are several rules for being safe on the Internet, but there
isn't much in the way of guidelines for interpersonal behavior. When
the boundaries become fuzzy and the rules change or get ignored, a
much higher degree of personal responsibility is needed. We are
challenged to rise up to create order in the world, starting with our
own choices and actions. As Janine pointed out in a recent e-mail
to me, "The rules for being decent and nice don't change on the
Internet."

While it is a bit of an "anything goes" situation on the Net, there
are some guidelines that can easily be surmised and followed. Those
that I have gleaned are spread throughout this book and that should
be helpful to you, but more important than my list of guidelines is
your own code of ethics.

🔲 **What do you stand for and what do you believe in? What are
your guiding values? Write them down as your own code of
ethics and actually use your personal code to guide your
behavior and choices. Take an opportunity to challenge your
own beliefs and values to be sure that you are really
committed to them.**

🔲 **What rules do you live by? Do these rules serve you?**

▦ Do your personal rules for life apply to your use of the Internet also?

Included in my own code of ethics is: to be respectful toward others and the planet, to be responsible, to have compassion, to live in authentic alignment, to be appreciative, and to be of service. My intent is for all of my efforts and communications to reflect these ethics.

If you discover a discrepancy between the way you behave in the world and the way you behave online, be watchful of how this affects your self-esteem and your relationships. If being honest is something you believe in, be sure you apply this value in both worlds. If being respectful of others' feelings is your preference, make an effort to be consistently respectful. Not only will you be doing the people you encounter—both online and off—a huge favor, you will also discover that living in alignment with your values and ethics is one of the keys to your heart.

PART TWO

Putting Yourself on the Line

"On the Internet, I win—smart, witty, fun to talk to. In the real world, dumb, thin, and pretty wins."

MELISSA, 38

"Since I have been online, I have become assertive, somewhat aggressive, and more outgoing. I have become more secure in who I am and I love the me that I have met."

MARTA, 38

"You learn more about yourself through other people's eyes. The way we can communicate online or in person can project our behavior in a light we would not ordinarily see."

PETE, 28

"It is important to know who you are and stick to it. It is easy to adopt a facade that is not an accurate representation of who you really are."

ALEXANDER, 48

"It's all about who you really are or how you see yourself, not about how you want other people to see you. You have to respect yourself online if you want anyone worth anything to respect you as well."

TESS, 34

4

The Freedom of Choice

HEN YOU LOG ON TO AN ONLINE DATING SERVICE, most of them require that you fill out their profile questionnaire before you can browse around their site—even for a free trial membership. Some of these questionnaires are brief, covering only basic information about you—age, sexual orientation, occupation, religion, race, marital status, physical build, geographic location, and education. Others take the questioning deeper, inquiring about hobbies, entertainment, astrological sign, personality attributes, political party, likes, and dislikes. The questionnaires will also inquire about your preferences for a partner and your relationship goals. Many of the online dating sites are equipped to do a computerized search for you, sorting through your preferences and other people's qualities to help you make a match.

While most of these questionnaires can be answered with one-word replies or multiple-choice options from which you can pick and choose, there are also essay questions on several of the sites that require more in-depth thought. When choosing a site, you may want to take the quality of the questionnaire into consideration. I recommend sites that offer essays, as they provide a lot of food for thought and are often the best source of information for distinguishing one person from the next.

The following essay topics, or slight variations thereof, are commonly found in some of the more thoughtful online questionnaires:

* Describe yourself (in 200 words or less)
* More about my perfect date…
* My perception of an ideal relationship…
* In my mind, the first date should be…
* This is what I've learned from my past relationships…
* Describe what turns you off.

> **What do you want? What don't you want? What do you have to offer? Practice answering the essay questions offline, when you have time to think.**

Most people pay close attention to what is said in the essays, as that is where individuality and creativity emerge. The questions and exercises strewn throughout this book will help you to clarify what you want to include in your profile. Since your responses to the essay questions could draw to you a potential life partner, it is worth putting some thought into them rather than answering off the top of your head. Answering the questions in a word processing program that has a spell checker and then cutting and pasting them into the site questionnaire is wise, as poor spelling can immediately cause someone to overlook an otherwise wonderful person.

Once completed, your profile will be posted on the site with thousands of others and you will then be able to enter the site. Just browsing through the sites, even if you have no intention of dating, is an amazing experience. You get an immediate sense of the huge numbers of people looking for a partner and the variety of types, interests, and lifestyles that this world holds. As you browse around, you will feel your own criteria for a partner emerging. Even the length of an essay answer may become a determinant for whether you are interested in someone or not. As I read through people's profiles, I found that if they answered with short or incomplete sentences, or used glib or sarcastic remarks, I didn't feel as if they were taking the task of finding a mate seriously and quickly moved on to someone else who was.

▣ Pay attention! What pulls you in? What pushes you away?

Reading people's profiles helps us to clarify what we are looking for in a partner. A woman in her 40s said, "Dating online has helped me to define the type of person and qualities that I want. I am also clearer about what I don't want and know that I don't have to settle for just anyone. I can break things off if I choose." This is a very powerful position to be in. Many people in the physical world of dating find themselves settling for whoever is available, operating from a sense of scarcity rather than abundance. In online dating, we quickly become aware of the tremendous number of people looking to connect. The downside of this is that, because of sheer numbers, we may dismiss people for superficial reasons—people with whom, if we had met face-to-face, we may have had a tremendous connection.

While you are considering your choices about what you want and don't want in a relationship, I am going to focus on laying some very important foundational skills that will help you in building *all* of your relationships, whether online or off. The ability to make powerful decisions, to practice self-observation, and to take personal responsibility will serve you throughout time if you continue to practice and apply them.

Choices Abound

One of the benefits of online dating is that it helps us to recognize that we have a lot of options. We can choose to be passive and wait for people to contact us. We can choose to be assertive and send an inquiry to a person who intrigues us. We can choose to delete a message or respond. We can choose to take what someone says seriously, or personally, or simply ignore it. We not only have choices about whom we date or marry, but we also have choices about how we behave and the quality that we bring to our relationships.

The good news is that choice is very powerful. The bad news—at least to some—is that choice requires responsibility. Personally, I like taking responsibility for myself and my life. I like knowing that if I don't enjoy something, I can respond to it in a new way and create a new situation. I like knowing that I am the author of my life and if I bring in a character who is a villain, I can "write" that person out or change the way that I interact with them, minimizing their impact on me. If I don't have enough love in my life, I can choose to be more loving. There is tremendous freedom in embracing that responsibility.

That we have choices seems obvious, but so often we get into difficult situations, and rather than recognizing that we can change what is happening in our lives, we get stuck. We get stuck when we think that what needs to change is the other person, or the situation, rather than our *response* to the other person or the events in our lives.

Debbie once came to me complaining about her boyfriend, Mark. Her list included how he was abusive, her kids hated him, and their whole family was in jeopardy over this relationship. When I asked why she was still seeing him, she replied that she was waiting for him to leave and so far, he hadn't. Waiting for Mark to make this move was causing Debbie to feel like a victim, not only because of his abusive behavior, but also because he wouldn't leave. This is the ultimate example of putting our power in someone else's hands. What Debbie wasn't realizing was that she didn't need to wait for Mark to leave; instead, *she* could leave the relationship. We need to take responsibility for our own well-being and that of our families. This is a matter of choice.

The Internet offers us a degree of ease in decision making. We are getting better at determining what we will and won't put up with and what we want and don't want in a relationship. However, because we are not face-to-face with the people we are talking to, often we don't have to deal with the consequences of our choices. If we don't write back to someone, or if we break up or say mean things via e-mail, we don't have to handle their hurt. We don't have to see the pain in their eyes. We can simply delete any further messages from them. This separation from the impact of our words and behavior on other people can cause us to disassociate from our responsibility for our actions. We need to be conscious about our choices and aware of the impact that we have on others, even if we can't see them.

As we become more practiced, via the Internet, in making choices about what we want, defining our comfort zones, and establishing our boundaries, we can bring those same skills into our everyday, face-to-face relationships. Imagine a world in which people are able to clearly articulate what they need and how they are feeling, let someone know when their feelings are hurt and clear it up right away, or stop a relationship immediately if it is not in alignment with their values! People are hungry for honest, clear communication. We are tired of the confusion of playing games, following arbitrary rules, and trying to second-guess what someone else is thinking. By becoming aware of the skills we are developing on the Internet and consciously applying them in the rest of our lives, we can make huge strides in creating healthier relationships.

What have you learned about yourself by interacting with others online?

This question is far more powerful than it first appears. No book or teacher can instill lessons like those you can learn yourself by taking a moment to self-reflect and pay attention to your own life experiences. Without taking that moment, however, you may not even realize what you are gaining. Throughout this book, you will find listings of what your fellow online dating members discovered about themselves as they answered this question. As you read their responses, consider how the world of relationships could be if all these lessons—learned from Internet interactions—were applied face-to-face. A few of their answers are given below:

"I have learned what I am really looking for in another person. Answering all of these endless questions about relationships caused me to think about it more than I had in the past and as the saying goes, 'you aren't going to find it if you don't know what you're looking for.' Now I know." —*Jill, 28*

"I've learned to always be myself and always be honest with the other person—after all, they are real." —*Ed, 46*

"No matter what, I still have to extend myself a little to meet new people." —*Michael, 35*

"I learned how to be more simple, more able to be understood by others, and saw my mistakes in trying to show off. I've found that the simpler my words and photos are and the more they come from the heart, the more they touch other people."
—*Gabe, 36*

"I can express myself better now." —*Cecile, 35*

"I rush into things too fast." —*Jake, 41*

"I've learned that in the past I've basically 'settled' and I will not do that again." —*Lisa, 41*

"I've learned to actually take the time to get to know someone."
—*Terry, 22*

"I cannot let the opinion of another change mine as far as how I feel about myself as a person. If I want to be treated courteously, I need to treat the people I meet in the same manner."
—*Greg, 41*

"When I read my own profiles, I have realized aspects of myself that I've never really noticed before. I am strong-minded and more independent than I thought and can attract really intelligent, professional people." —*Annie, 24*

"I've learned to express myself to people from other countries and be understood without being offensive." —*Toby, 35*

"Online dating has made me less nervous about meeting new people. I've learned that my gut feeling about a person is usually right on." —*Julia, 53*

"I've learned the importance of honesty at the beginning of a relationship." —*Don, 63*

"I've learned that I have a good personality, a good sense of humor, and that people really do like me for who I am, not just for my looks! I'm much more outgoing." —*Patricia, 44*

"Make the first move; you've got nothing to lose." —*Todd, 32*

"I'm not desperate." —*Gail, 40*

"I have learned to listen to other people's opinions." —*Larry, 34*

"Online dating helped me to dig down deep and figure out what I was looking for and what makes me 'tick.'" —*Margaret, 37*

▦ How can you apply what you've learned about yourself to your face-to-face relationships?

Keep in mind that what you learn from your experience is also your choice. While one person will say with hope, "I realized I am not alone in my search," another will choose to say, "I am one of billions of lonely people and will be alone forever." While one person will say, "I have learned to be discerning about who I trust," another will choose to say, "I learned not to trust." Look at your personal "lessons" and see if they need to be restated to more accurately reflect what you want to create in your life. Our language is very powerful. *If you don't want to be lonely, don't create loneliness with your mind-set and word choices.* Become aware of what you are thinking and, in any given moment, reframe the situation to be in alignment with what you want to create.

Event + Response
= Outcome and Solution (EROS)

"The new playful Eros means that impulses and modes from other spheres
enter the relations between men and women."
— HERBERT GOLD

In *Intellectual Foreplay*, I discuss the equation "Event + Response = Outcome," which I learned from Jack Canfield, coauthor of the *Chicken Soup for the Soul* series, and then adapted and expanded for use with relationships. Event + Response = Outcome and Solution is so valuable it is worth repeating here. What E + R = OS means is that an event is *what is;* we have very little, if any, control over the events of our lives. We are generally powerless to change events because the minute they happen, they are in the past, no longer changeable, and they are often a result of other people's behavior, over which we have no control. Therefore, what makes or breaks the outcome or our experience is the addition of our *response to* that event. By *choosing a response* that is in alignment with the outcome that we want to bring about, we make ourselves very powerful. As long as we are only trying to change the *event,* we are powerless.

This recognition of choice is the very quality that allows someone to take a really challenging circumstance, overcome it, and end up making huge contributions to society with the wisdom that they share. Someone who does not understand the power of choice ends up feeling like a victim to the circumstances of life. Powerlessness takes over and depression sets in. The result is not caused by the event; it is caused by the response to that event. In any case, we are responsible for the outcome that we create.

In relationships, this equation, Event + Response = Outcome and Solution, is particularly powerful. The "event" can be looked at as your partner's (or *any* other person in your life) beliefs and behaviors: the Other Person + Your Response to the Other Person = Your Experience. We have no control over another person and their behavior. *Our power is entirely in our choice of responses to the other person or the event.*

> ▨ **Think about any event in your life. How did you respond to it? What other responses could you have chosen that would have created different results?**

Putting E + R = OS into Practice

Dan and Jean, a married couple, came to see me because they were having problems. She had had an online affair with a guy, Brian, that had turned into a real sexual encounter, and now Dan and Jean were wondering what to do. After they told their story, we identified the "event" to be the affair. Now they needed to decide how they wanted to respond to that event, creating the outcome of their situation. Their first thought was that maybe they should get divorced. I suggested that they put that option aside for the time being and consider *what they would choose to do if divorce were not an option.*

I explained that we really only have four response options when an event happens or when we encounter a certain behavior or belief in another person:

1. We can to **negotiate** to change the other person's behavior or the event.

2. We can **resist** the other person or the event and stay in the relationship.

3. We can **accept** the other person's behavior or the event and stay in the relationship.

4. We can **get out** of the relationship.

Negotiation is a valid place to start; however, we have no control over what another person chooses to do. To negotiate is an effort to change the event, or the other person. They may be *willing* to alter their behavior, but that has to be their decision. In this case, Jean had already stopped seeing or communicating with Brian, but the issue of having the same thing happen again was still a concern for both of them.

What most of us end up doing when we encounter something that we don't like is to *resist* what has happened or resist the other person. By resist, I mean that we get upset about it or complain about it. We often talk behind the other person's back, make sarcastic comments, or get insulting or manipulative by whining or threatening. When we go into resistance, we get locked into control battles in which there are no winners. The choice to resist the other person always leads to killing the love in the relationship. Resistance leads to resentment and resentment leads to revenge. Jean's decision to have an affair in the first place was undoubtedly due to her resistance to Dan and something that was happening in their relationship. However, her chosen response did not bring about the desired outcome of improving the situation.

When we begin resisting the other person by making sarcastic comments or put-downs, we are hoping the other person will "get a clue" and change their behavior. Resistance is really *an unskilled attempt to negotiate for change.* We think if we drop enough hints or make enough criticisms the other person will "get it" and behave differently. It very seldom works that way! Usually, the person just gets angry and then finds ways to get even. Because we focused on changing the other person or the event, we are once again rendered powerless. If Dan chose to stay in the relationship but proceeded to belittle Jean, making snide or sarcastic comments, their relationship would stand no chance.

The third response option requires changing *yourself* instead of the event or other person. Acceptance doesn't mean that Dan would have to find Jean's behavior acceptable *in his life,* but rather that he accepts that Jean is who she is, and that the event, or affair, happened. Again, we have no control over changing the event.

By accepting *what is,* you are free to make a decision about what *you* want to do about it. From a place of acceptance, you may decide to stay in the relationship, continuing to explore ways to make things better and addressing the issues with a solution-focused attitude. If you choose to respond to the event by staying in the relationship, doing so from a place of acceptance of the other person will lead to a healthy and loving situation. However, it may be that, while you accept that this event took place or that the other person is the way they are, it is unacceptable for you to stay in a relationship with them.

If you cannot negotiate to change the circumstances, and you know that resistance will kill the love in the relationship, and you cannot accept your partner's behavior, then option number four, getting out, is the only one remaining.

Jean and Dan considered this for a while. Since the event had already taken place, they could not negotiate to change it. Jean had already stopped seeing and communicating with Brian, so that didn't need to be addressed further. Neither Jean nor Dan wanted to live a soap opera existence, so they chose not to go into a state of resistance to one another. This left either accepting the circumstances and each other and looking for solutions within their relationship, or getting out of the marriage.

As I said earlier, their first reaction was to get out, but once I asked what they would do if divorce were not an option, they started exploring other possibilities. They decided that rather than get out of the relationship, they would prefer to look at the situation, see if they could figure out what had led to Jean's looking outside of their relationship for companionship, and choose different behaviors in their marriage to make it stronger. They came up with a list of things that they were going to actively work on, individually and together.

I am not trying to imply that moving on is an easy thing to do when something like this happens in a relationship. Rather, I'm saying that if you have a certain goal or outcome that you want to create, how you respond to events will be what determines whether or not you reach your goals. Taking some time to consider your options, rather than merely reacting, will empower you tremendously. Dan and Jean were reacting when they immediately thought about getting divorced. By taking the time to step back and consider other options, they were able to choose responses that were in alignment with the goal of saving their marriage.

This $E + R = OS$ equation can be applied to every situation you encounter. If someone e-mails you a nasty note, that is the event. If someone fails to reply to your advances, that is also an event. How you choose to respond is up to you. If someone sends you a love letter asking you to marry them, that is also an event to which you can choose how to respond.

> **By carefully choosing your responses instead of just reacting to the events around you, you can create solutions that are in alignment with your goals.**

No More Playing the Blame Game

Regardless of what we are doing in our lives—working, playing, fighting, accomplishing—at one time or another, most of us wonder what it all means and whether there is something more to life than just participating in it. When we experience unfortunate or painful events, it is common for us to hear, "Look for the lesson in this. There must be a reason." As a society, we are slowly but surely learning to respond with a bit more patience to "bad" events, trusting—or perhaps *hoping*—that if we just wait, the "silver lining" will be revealed. . . and quite often it is.

The strange thing is that, when it comes to love, rather than looking within to see the lesson, we tend to look outside of ourselves for the reasons things happen the way they do. When we look outside ourselves for the reasons, we end up assigning blame. When we blame circumstances outside of ourselves, we give up our power and become victims, rather than taking responsibility for what we are creating. I call this "the blame game."

Jean could easily have blamed Dan for not paying enough attention to her and Dan could easily have blamed Jean for not being faithful. From there, the accusations would have flown, back and forth, building only more anger. Instead, Jean took responsibility for the choices she had made and the impact they had on her marriage. Dan also reflected on the choices he had made that had contributed to what happened. As a result, they were freed to move forward creatively, constructively. By taking responsibility for our own actions, we are empowered to create different results.

Sharon met a man, Ron, online and immediately liked what she saw. They arranged to meet in person and ended up spending the night together the first weekend that they met. When she didn't hear from him afterwards, she began blaming him, calling him names, and blaming online dating for only having "jerks." She felt victimized by both Ron and the dating service.

After Sharon finished venting, we discussed what her part in the situation was. Reluctantly, she came to see that she hadn't taken the time to get to know Ron before getting so seriously involved. Because she didn't consider herself to be a person who participated in "casual sex," once she had sex with Ron, she talked to him about commitment so that he would know she "wasn't like *that.*" Now, as she examined her own behavior, she began to see that her desire to be monogamous probably came across as desperation. She could see how the things she had said and done—and the order in which she did them—might have scared him away.

The "downside" to taking responsibility is that we have no one to blame. This is not to imply that Ron didn't have a responsibility—he certainly did—but Sharon is ultimately responsible for her own behavior. If my conversation had been with Ron instead, I would hope that he too would have realized that he hadn't taken the time see if his own and Sharon's expectations were in alignment before they slept together. The problem could have been avoided and a nice relationship might have developed, if they had taken their time and used their heads before sharing their bodies.

The upside of taking responsibility is that we begin to see how powerful we are in creating the experiences we encounter. Responsibility sometimes feels like a double-edged sword, requiring us to have a higher level of integrity and to be accountable for ourselves. It also empowers us to see that we have an active role in creating the life and the love we want to have. By taking responsibility we are able to make new choices and avoid recreating the same problem again and again.

Self-Observation

Choosing *wise* responses to the events in our lives requires certain skills. First, we need to develop the art of self-observation. Second, we need to identify our values and goals so that we can make choices that are likely to help us realize them. In Chapter 3 we explored your code of ethics and goals for online dating, and we'll go even further into this in Part Three: "Making Contact." For now, let's focus on what self-observation is all about.

Self-observation is a tremendously valuable skill that can be applied every moment of your life, from your virtual reality to your daily existence. Self-observation is the ability to take a step back and look at yourself from a different perspective, as if you were taking a snapshot and examining your own behavior. This is as simple as asking yourself:

* What am I doing right now?
* How am I feeling right now?
* Are the actions that I am choosing aligned with my goals?

By doing this, you will be able to recognize unconscious choices that you are making in different situations. Once you recognize this, you can make conscious choices about what, if anything, you would like to do differently. David, a man in his 30s, sent me an e-mail telling me all about how he had gotten involved with a woman online because she had a "kind face." She lived hundreds of miles away in another state, but he pursued the relationship anyhow. After months of trying to negotiate the distance, they eventually broke up, in part because neither of them was in a position to move.

A few months later, David began corresponding with another woman who had responded to his profile, but she also lived far away. I suggested that, rather than just embarking on a new relationship, David pull back and observe himself first. What was he doing? What did he want? Why did he think this situation would have a different result than the last? David realized he was heading into the exact same scenario that he had painfully just ended. So he wrote back to the woman, letting her know he appreciated her interest but wasn't in the market for a long-distance relationship. Often, just a single moment of self-observation can cause us to choose an entirely different path than the one we are currently on.

Another benefit of self-observation is that, by observing our lives, we are able to see our *selves* as different from our *behavior.* Our actions are not *who we are;* rather they are *what we choose to do.* When we observe ourselves, we see ourselves from another perspective and can identify with the aspect of ourselves that is the observer, not just the observed. We identify with the aspect of ourselves that is responsible for *choosing* our actions. We recognize that there is a part of our being that is not attached to the drama of our emotions or embroiled in the ego's battle for control or approval. Instead, the "witness" is calm, strong, and able to see the bigger picture. This witness self is in a much better position to make wise decisions because from this bird's-eye view of our lives, we can not only see where we are, but also where we want to go. From this perspective, we can see which choices of behavior will lead us there.

You will find self-observation a very useful tool while dating or relating. By practicing and refining your abilities in this area, you will gain a deeper sense of your own strength and your ability to make powerful choices.

▨ Throughout your day, practice self-observation: simply stop and become aware of what you are doing and how you are feeling in any given moment.

▨ Consider your goals in terms of the quality of relationships that you desire and the outcomes that you want to create. Are your daily actions aligned with your goals? If not, take a few deep breaths and then choose new actions.

5

Mirror, Mirror

J ORDAN IS A YOUNG MAN who enjoys online dating because he can be anyone he wants to be. In his "real" life, he is shy and antisocial, but in e-mail and in chat rooms his normal inhibitions fall away. On the Internet, Jordan can be assertive, talkative, funny, and charming. The problem starts when the women he is conversing with want to meet in person, expecting to find someone with the same qualities that he displayed online. Jordan knows that his persona online and his persona in the flesh are not aligned— and he far prefers his online personality.

For Jordan, realizing that his online personality is no less real than his in-the-flesh personality is the first step. Jordan can express himself in many ways in different mediums. However, the difference between his online and offline personalities is a sign of low self-esteem. If he is capable of both personality styles and even prefers one over the other, there are underlying reasons why he isn't expressing the more social aspect of his personality in face-to-face situations.

Often it is a fear of judgement, or a need for approval, that stops us from taking risks or putting ourselves in front of others. Sometimes the cause is a lack of skill, as communicating in one arena requires a different skill set than communicating in another. In either case, learning new skills—either interpersonal or self-esteem enhancing—can remedy the situation.

By observing which aspects of his personality he has access to online and consciously practicing bringing those out in his face-to-face interactions, Jordan can learn to integrate his online personality with his real-world personality. He wouldn't be able to access this outgoing facet of his personality so easily online unless he already had that quality within him. All he really needs to do is unbury it and practice a little. Doing this is just like building any other skill, whether pitching a baseball or learning to be polite.

By contrast, some people who are very nice and social in the real world allow their "evil twin" to come out on the Net, taking advantage of the anonymity to let their darker side out to play. This, too, is a self-esteem issue, as we are about to explore. Part Five: "Moving from Virtual to Physical" will address the challenges that not being aligned can present in terms of *dating,* but first let's look at the problems these discrepancies create within us in terms of self-esteem.

Self-Esteem

I define "self-esteem" as "knowing our true essence *and* living in alignment with that essence." Since I maintain that our essence is love, we display our self-esteem when we are living in alignment with our loving, compassionate selves. A false sense of self-esteem is when one's core values (or lack thereof) are damaging to oneself and society, in which case professional help is needed. In this discussion, I'll be referring to healthy self-esteem and socially accepted values.

In a normal, mentally stable person, when there is a gap between what we believe in and how we act, the size of the gap is an indicator of how we feel about ourselves. Essentially, the wider the gap, the lower one's self-esteem. The more aligned our actions are with our values, the higher our self-esteem. For example, if you value honesty but regularly tell lies, there is a wide gap, which indicates low self-esteem. The definition of "integrity," according to *Webster's,* is "behavior in accordance with a strict code of values." Hence, when you have defined your values and personal code of ethics and actively live in alignment with them, you are living with integrity. Your self-esteem, which is closely related to integrity, can blossom.

Ultimately, one of our main tasks as human beings is to align our outer self with our inner self. The world of self-improvement is booming because millions of people are seeking such wholeness: alignment between their heads and their hearts, their behaviors and their goals, their physical being and their spiritual being. Not surprisingly, an equally strong push is that to find our soul mate, a partner with whom our soul is in alignment. As I said before, however, in order to find your soul mate, you must be living in alignment with your own soul. Otherwise, partners meet gap-to-gap instead of soul-to-soul. Meeting gap-to-gap forms a hole that a relationship can fall through if you're not careful. Meeting line-to-line forms a strong and powerful path on which the relationship can proceed and grow. Nothing is more stimulating than two people meeting without games and rules and roles—just two open hearts ready and willing to play and progress.

▓ Evaluate your own self-esteem. How do you feel about yourself? How confident are you about dating and relating?

Aligning your virtual self or online personality with your real self will also help to close the gap and raise your self-esteem. Many people told me that dating online helped them to feel better about themselves. One woman in her 30s wrote, "I have learned via online dating to be able talk about myself with confidence again." Another in her 20s said, "Online dating makes me feel better about myself, especially when I check my e-mail box and it is full of mail from guys that are interested!" A man in his 40s added, "I found that I am more datable than I thought," and someone else said, "I'm a better communicator than I had realized."

The process of filling out online dating questionnaires causes you to look at yourself from the perspective of your good qualities and what you have to offer. To answer the questions, you are virtually forced into a state of self-observation. Kristina, a woman in her 40s, explained, "As I filled out the questionnaire, I had to explain my wishes and favors *to myself*, because I had to describe them."

The process of filling out questionnaires, however, also makes a lot of people uncomfortable. We are generally not well practiced at identifying and sharing our good qualities. When asked about our strengths, we also encounter self-judgment. When asked to identify her successes, a woman in one of my workshops couldn't think of a single accomplishment. When I pointed out to her that she had a Ph.D., a significant professional and academic achievement, she replied, "Oh, that doesn't count because it took me too long to get it."

Self-judgement stops us from accepting and sharing some of our best qualities and accomplishments. If you find yourself having a hard time sharing your strengths and skills, practice self-observation, pay attention to how you are feeling, take some deep breaths, and try again. If revealing good news about yourself doesn't come easily, practice!

⊠ **What are your good qualities? What do you have to offer in a relationship?**

⊠ **What are the good qualities or accomplishments that friends, colleagues, or family have recognized you for? Do you value or discount these qualities and accomplishments?**

People also feel discomfort when there is a discrepancy between how they see themselves and how they want the world to view them. One woman explained, "As I filled out the questionnaire, I felt I was going to be judged 'on paper' and I didn't look as good there as I do in real life. Everyone carries weight differently. Although I am 20 pounds overweight, I am voluptuous and proportionate. If I fill out the height and weight fields accurately, I sound short and fat.

However, in person I get a lot of attention because I look pretty good. My dilemma is whether I should lie about my weight—and be dishonest—or tell the truth and risk scaring people away." She went on, "If I further describe my figure as shapely in my essay, then I'm going to have all these guys making sexual comments. I don't want to lie, but the truth leaves too much room for misconceptions. Either way is uncomfortable."

Here are some steps that can guide you out of discomfort when you recognize a gap between who you are and how you show up:

1. Remember who you *really* are and what you want.

2. Self-observe.

3. Choose actions in alignment with your personal code of ethics and the results you want to create.

By observing where you are now and knowing where you want to go, you can choose the actions and words that will get you there. Following your own code of ethics will help you achieve your goals with integrity, which, in itself, will raise your self-esteem.

When I went to my very first self-esteem workshop, taught by Jack Canfield, he had us do an exercise that I will now pass on to you.

1. Close your eyes and imagine that you are looking at your own mirrored image.

2. Look deeply into your own eyes and say to yourself, "I love you and accept you just the way you are."

3. Watch for the reaction in your mirrored image. Pay attention to how you feel saying and receiving this message of self-love.

4. What was your reaction to this exercise? Did it feel good? Did it feel uncomfortable? Were you willing to try it?

When I did as Jack instructed, I was greatly surprised. My image rolled her eyes at me and said, "Yeah, sure you do," *very* sarcastically. I was floored. Until that moment, I was unaware that I had a self-esteem issue. For some of you, doing this exercise probably felt good. For others, it was undoubtedly painful, as it was for me the first time. In either case, *your feelings are a blessing.* If the mirror exercise felt good, your blessing is your strong self-esteem. If it was painful, your gift is the knowledge that your self-esteem needs tending to, and you can now take steps toward doing this. As long as you are unconscious about how you feel, as I was, you won't do anything to improve your self-esteem. Once I was given this gift, I embraced the opportunity to do everything in my power to turn things around. I began studying, practicing, and applying self-esteem-enhancing techniques and philosophies, and eventually began teaching them so that I could help others as well. The gift of that uncomfortable and painful moment set me firmly on the path of my life's purpose.

If you wish to raise your self-esteem, start by doing the mirror exercise in a real mirror every morning and evening. Looking into your own eyes, tell yourself what you like, love, admire, and appreciate about yourself and end with telling yourself that you love yourself. Continue this every day until it becomes comfortable and habitual.

While the mirror exercise may seem narcissistic, the point is not to become conceited but to switch your automatic habit of seeing negative things about yourself when you look into the mirror to seeing and acknowledging your positive, lovable qualities. You will not be able to receive positive attention and compliments from other people, or believe them, if you cannot recognize those qualities in yourself. Self-esteem and conceit are not the same thing. Conceit pushes people away, while self-esteem attracts them.

When you venture out to meet new people, feeling good about your strengths always puts you in a more powerful position. Low self-esteem is not an attractive trait. If you don't like yourself, your words will leak this truth to the people you are trying to attract. Practicing acknowledging your strengths in the mirror will translate to the way you present yourself in questionnaires and e-mail, and in verbal conversations as well.

Also, as you look into your own eyes, you will come to know another aspect of yourself, beyond the physical being you normally see in the mirror. As the saying goes, "The eyes are the window to the soul." When we talk to other people, if they do not make eye contact we often think that something is wrong or that they are lying to us. We don't feel connected. However, we seldom establish this kind of soul connection with ourselves—so try it; you might like it!

Self-Talk

In addition to being conscious about what we say to ourselves when we look in a mirror, we need to be aware of what we say to ourselves all day long. So many of us have the nasty habit of bombarding ourselves with hundreds of negative comments in a day. We tell ourselves that we are ugly, stupid, fat, unlovable, no good, unworthy, and so on. This constant barrage of put-downs wears down our self-esteem. It lessens our ability to choose appropriate responses, take necessary risks, and create the outcomes we really want, so we fulfil our negative prophesies instead.

This is hardly the mind-set with which to search for our life partner! One man, Dale, wrote, "I'm never going to meet someone." With this as his mantra, he is probably right. Henry Ford once said, "Whether you think you can or think you can't, you are right." Our words, attitudes, and beliefs are far more powerful than we realize.

Indeed, self-talk can give us valuable feedback, but often what we tell ourselves isn't actually true. It reflects a *self-defeating belief system* instead. If we aren't aware that these beliefs are affecting us, we can't do anything to turn the situation around.

During the course of the day, whenever you hear your internal "tape" running, simply observe what is being said and consider how you want to respond. At any given moment, self-observation provides a mirror that reflects back to us what we need to see and the choices that are available to us.

Remember the power of choice and the response options that we talked about in the last chapter—E + R = OS? The same options apply to turning your self-esteem and self-talk around. If you find that you are silently or verbally putting yourself down, consider that situation to be the *event* to which you need to *respond*. You can choose to *negotiate* with yourself to change what you are saying or doing—which may or may not work. You can choose to continue criticizing yourself, believe every word, and sabotage your life. Or, you can actively work on self-acceptance and self-love, choosing to accept that an internal dialog of criticism is playing, and *laughing* at the words instead of believing them.

This last option is my personal choice. Sometimes, in the middle of speaking to several hundred people, I become aware of a tape running in my head. I'll hear, "That was a stupid thing to say" or "You're boring that guy; he's falling asleep!" Rather than becoming upset and believing the criticism, I laugh at the dynamic that allows me to talk out loud about self-esteem while still hearing critical messages inside myself. This is a matter of choosing what you want to honor. I choose to honor my deeper knowledge that I am a good teacher, capable of sharing valuable information.

Unlike the options we have when dealing with others, "getting out" of a relationship with oneself is *never* an option. Some people turn to substance abuse or suicide, mistakenly thinking that they can escape from themselves. As the saying goes, "no matter where you go, there you are." Channeling your energy into self-awareness and acceptance will bring you far greater rewards than trying to escape.

Allow the world of online dating to be a mirror that reflects to you that which you need to pay attention to in your life.

One woman in her late 30s said, "Online dating has helped me find more positive things about myself and it is starting to come easier. I used to write a lot of negatives about myself." As you become aware of your self-talk and the way you describe yourself in online questionnaires or e-mails, pay attention to the words you use. If you think you need to lie to be attractive to others, if you can't identify your strengths, or if you find you don't know yourself well enough to honestly answer the questions, recognize this as a gift. Again, the gift is that you are being shown an area of your life that needs your attention. You can now either choose to ignore it and continue to let your low self-esteem affect your life and your relationships, or you can choose to actively develop your self-esteem. It is up to you.

> **What kinds of words do you use to describe yourself? What do you mean by those words? What message are you sending to other people?**

Live Your Life!

As you practice self-observation, you will begin to recognize when you feel uncomfortable with something someone says or with one of your own thoughts. When this happens, *pay attention!* If something you read online excites you or makes you hopeful, pay attention to *what is said,* not just to who you think is saying it. Until you have actually met the person you are talking to, your feelings about what is said are a more accurate reflection of *you* than of the other person. Since the honesty issue is a definite challenge in anonymous interactions, initially your most accurate and useful information will be what you learn about yourself.

Cynthia, a woman in her 50s, told me: "Following your advice, as I paid attention to what I was feeling as I interacted with people online, I began to see patterns about what mattered to me. When someone would talk to me about spirituality, I would get really engaged. The same was true when they shared their goals and future dreams. I began to see the value that I place on having a sense of purpose and direction." Gary, a man in his 30s, said, "The thing I kept finding myself keying into were people's career goals. I guess that reflects where I am in my life right now. I'm pretty driven and motivated to succeed."

The same holds true as you skim through profiles or personal ads. Which qualities and activities do you find yourself drawn to? I remember once feeling like I was falling in love with a guy in a personals ad as I read about building bonfires on the beach and watching the sunset transition into night. As I began yearning for the person who placed the ad, I suddenly realized that it wasn't *the person* that I was yearning for, but rather the activities and *the quality of life* that he was describing. There was no person yet to yearn for—only words on a page that anyone could have written.

> ▨ **As you read through the profiles online, make a list of what intrigues you and actively begin incorporating those activities into your life now, with or without a partner.**

The activities and qualities that you list are those keys to your heart that I mentioned earlier in this book. There is no need to wait for someone else to do what you love to do. In fact, you will probably find that the more you get out of your house to do what you love, the more you will encounter people in your real life who love the same things. If you are looking for an "active, outdoorsy kind of person," it always helps to *be* an "active, outdoorsy kind of person," so you will be attractive to the other person as well.

The Internet is a viable way to meet people—lots of people. But it is *one way, not the only way.* A friend of mine said that she sometimes spent as many as 5 hours a day, 7 days a week, reading through profiles, chatting, and e-mailing in her search for a mate. When I mentioned a beautiful beach community 5 minutes from her home, she said had never been there. My friend was spending so much time in her virtual world, she was missing out on real-life activities with physical human beings in her own home town. *Virtual reality has its place, without a doubt, but don't let it replace your reality.* After all, it always helps to have an interesting life to share when you do meet your match!

Putting What You Love into Words

In addition to paying attention to what intrigues you in the activities, qualities, and words that other people use, pay attention to your own words as you share them with others. Are your words congruent with the relationship you want to create? As Nancy realized, "What I really wanted to find on the Internet was a man with whom I could build a long-lasting relationship, someone who really cared about me. But as I became aware of my own words, I realized that I was trying to lure men in with sexual innuendoes, which always led our conversations to a place where I began to get uncomfortable. At some point, I had to take responsibility for some of the superficiality or the direction of the conversation. I mean, some of these guys may never have taken the conversation in that direction if I hadn't said something that started it."

Nancy went on to tell me how she realized, simply by observing herself, that her pattern of being sexual too early in a relationship arose in online relationships, just as it did in real life. From that moment of awareness forward, Nancy chose to lead the conversations in a direction that was in alignment with where she wanted her relationships to go.

Lani, 57, had a similar realization. "I want to be true to myself, so I never lean toward making my profile into something teasing and seductive, for fear of getting the wrong kind of attention. It is bad enough as it is. I usually state in my profile, 'Please guys, no marrieds, no pen pals, no answering on a whim....'"

◈ **Pay attention to what you choose to say in your online communications. How do you feel as you are saying it? Are you being congruent with your values?**

I'm hoping that you have been taking notes on your answers to the questions that have been posed to you. As you practice writing your essay answers for the online questionnaires, reread your notes to be sure that what you love about yourself and about life are reflected in your writing! Not only will the process of signing onto Internet dating sites reveal to you valuable information about yourself, it will also provide an opportunity to reflect the good news about yourself in your writing for a prospective sweetheart. Let your words be the ones that stir his or her soul!

6

A Picture Is Worth a Thousand Words

WHEN I GO TO A BOOKSTORE to find a book, I don't feel comfortable buying it if the cover does not have a picture of the author. I like to see an author's picture to get a sense of their essence—the impression that comes through their eyes, not from their features. I look for congruence between the message and the messenger. If someone looks mean or scary to me, I may not want to buy his book on peaceful living. If someone looks unbalanced, I won't want to buy her book on spirituality. If someone looks out of shape, I won't buy his book on fitness! People who are dating online often feel much the same way. If you don't post a picture, most people will skip right over your profile and move on to the profiles in which they can see a photo. Some will even do a search requesting that the computer sort out any profiles that don't have pictures, so that they don't have to waste their time.

If you are serious about making a match online, get an accurate picture of yourself—literally and figuratively—and share it in your profile. In this chapter, we'll talk about how to present your physical image online and how this decision can lead you to self-discovery. Certainly, pictures can be very revealing, and in more ways than one! A 60-year-old woman, Patricia, said, "There was a man from California who came to Colorado where I live on a regular basis and wanted to meet someone to do things with. I thought, 'Sure, he is probably married,' but we chatted via e-mail a couple of times and he sent a new photo each time. The third e-mail included a nude shot of him getting into the shower and showed all essential parts! I explained to him that although I found him very attractive, I preferred a man who respected himself more than that. A nice body with half a brain is not even half the man I'm looking for!"

Sharing pictures online goes straight to the heart of our emotions: it opens up issues about body image, self-talk, and self-confidence. Pictures can stir feelings of interest, attraction, resentment, or rejection. As such, pictures are an easy area for deception. People who otherwise are very honest can be drawn to using pictures that are outdated, unrealistic, and, in some cases, not even of themselves. Other people, for various reasons, don't post them at all.

Intentionally posting a false picture is not playing fair. However, when viewing others' photos, keep in mind that not everyone has an accurate self-image. Rather than trying to be deceptive, they may post an outdated picture without realizing how their looks or physique have changed since their 20s (or 30s or 40s). Other people use a "glamour" or "GQ" shot with their profile, when in everyday life they don't look nearly as polished. As you decide which picture or pictures to post of yourself, I suggest using this reality check: when your e-date first meets you, they should not feel deceived. Deception is never a good place to start a relationship. Ask your friends or family to help you find a picture that accurately represents you, if you are having a hard time assessing for yourself.

Gloria, a woman in her 20s, had this strategy: "I posted a picture that didn't look quite as good as I do in person. I figured that if someone contacted me, satisfied with the way I looked in that picture, then they would be even more pleased with the real me."

⊠ **Have you posted or do you intend to post your picture online?**

⊠ **Is the picture you are posting accurate and up-to-date? If not, what is the underlying issue that your choice reveals to you? Are you trying to hide something? What? Why?**

Another regular complaint I hear is about people who don't post a picture at all. The common assumption is that if someone doesn't post a picture, they are either very unattractive or hiding from "America's Most Wanted." However, these assumptions may be far from accurate. I've heard several interesting reasons people have for choosing not to post their pictures.

Several women mentioned that their picture drew such a huge response, they didn't have time to answer all the respondents, so they took it offline. Contrary to the "too ugly" theory, these women were too attractive to have their pictures posted. Other people have told me that they don't want their friends and family to know they are dating online.

A female lawyer didn't like the thought of someone being able to download her picture off the Net. "Once you put it on the Net, you have no control over where it goes." One women didn't want her old boyfriend to know anything more about her, while another said her ex-husband was stalking her and so she didn't want her online picture attached to any information about her. There are also the married or involved folks who don't want anyone to see them online lest they get caught.

Lastly, some people say that they simply don't have a good picture of themselves available, but I find that a cop out. Taking a representative picture of yourself just isn't that hard. If you encounter this excuse, ask yourself what the underlying issues are.

When you find an intriguing profile without a picture, the best way to find out what the scoop is is to ask, "Why don't you have a picture with your profile?" While some may be dishonest, you may also receive a candid response.

One woman, Sherry, explained that she had to take her picture off the Net because she was getting many responses, but none of them referred to what she said about herself, only to how she looked. When Sherry took down her picture, she received fewer responses, *but the quality of the content was higher.* Sherry's is an excellent example of taking responsibility for the kind of outcome you desire. Rather than assuming "all men are after one thing," Sherry considered what she could do differently to draw a different response, and then she followed through.

▣ **What does the picture you have posted say about you?**

▣ **What kind of response have you gotten from it?**

▣ **What do you look for in someone else's picture?**

No matter how much we enjoy appreciation for our appearance, we want to know that we are cared about for deeper, more substantial reasons than just looks. We want to know our partner loves more than an aspect of ourselves that could fade and will change with time. As Tanya declared, "It is so nice to know that people like me without even seeing what I look like!" Of course, this can be deceptive, because sometimes they stop "liking you" as soon as they see your picture. One 50-year-old man shared sadly, "After dozens of e-mails and chats that got progressively warmer, we finally decided to exchange photos. Previously, there had been talk of the lady attending a convention in my hometown. I truthfully described myself as not pretty, but clean-cut. As soon as she got my photo, her reply was, 'Nice mustache, but sorry, you are not my type.' That was that." He offered this advice: "Try to keep your head. You may like everything about the other person, then find one huge turnoff."

Several people indicated that they liked getting away from the physical reality of society—having to look a certain way to be accepted. Jane explained that she loved the freedom that talking to a person with no picture offered. "I like getting away from the unspoken requirement to only talk to good-looking people when you're out dating. It is pretty great that even if you're not that good-looking, you still have a chance to meet interesting people." Another woman described online communication as an opportunity to talk "soul-to-soul" without bodies getting in the way. A man said, however, that he found this aspect to be disconcerting. "It is sort of like a séance, talking to a disembodied spirit. More chilling than warm and fuzzy."

If you decide not to post a picture of yourself, it would be helpful to briefly explain why. Respectfully explain your position in your own style. For example, "I'd like to introduce myself without my picture to see if we have anything other than the physical in common, and then let's go from there." Or, "Trying to keep my private life private, therefore not posting a picture. Will be happy to exchange photos with you as soon as we've established potential interest." Or, "I'm not wanted by the law; I just don't post my photo publicly." Including a brief description of your physical self will be helpful to those looking at your profile, and the process of writing this description is a good exercise for you, as well.

How Do You Describe Yourself Physically?

Describing our looks presents a challenge in itself. If we like the way we look, we may be concerned about sounding boastful or conceited in our description. If we don't like the way we look, describing ourselves without putting ourselves down is hard to do. Most of us can find a few of our features that we like. If you cannot, it is another one of those gifts appearing in your life, a golden opportunity to do some esteem-enhancing and self-acceptance exercises or to start taking better care of yourself.

When describing ourselves, we often resort to sharing what other people have said about us or refer to celebrities we think we resemble. This, however, isn't always accurate. Todd, a 22-year-old, exclaimed, "One woman wrote describing herself as looking like Jennifer Love Hewitt, but when we met she looked more like Rosie O'Donnell." He might have been completely happy with a Rosie look-alike, had that been what he was expecting. If you're going to describe yourself using someone else's likeness, be sure you are accurate!

▣ **Write a description of your physical self, then read it as if you were a stranger. Does it sound as if you like your body? Does it sound as if you are comfortable with the way you look?**

My description would sound like this: "I have a big smile and bluish green eyes. I have very curly blond hair, which always has that wind-blown (uncontrollable) look. I'm 5'4" and am eternally in need of more exercise than I allow myself to get. However, I am proportionate in size. If I had been born in another century, I would have made a great statue. One thing I particularly appreciate about my body is its strength and grace."

Whether you decide to post a description of yourself or never share it with others, the process of looking at and describing what you like about yourself, and being truthful about it, is excellent for all of us. It reveals both what we are comfortable and pleased with and those aspects we need to work on accepting or improving. Consider doing two descriptions of yourself. Write a private one for your eyes only that covers your whole body, then write a shorter one that you would be comfortable posting online. If you are planning to share your description online, be sure to consider the nature of the response you seek to evoke. Putting your measurements online, or saying that your best feature is your breasts or butt, will undoubtedly evoke a very sexual response from your online audience. That is fine if that is what you want, but take responsibility for this part of the process.

Body Image

Body image is one of the most common self-esteem issues for most people—which is usually why the truth about online photos is so varied. When we look in the mirror, we usually look directly at the things that we don't like and have judgmental thoughts about them. We assume that if this is what we first notice about ourselves, surely it must be what everyone else sees. This is a self-defeating process, much like the negative self-talk we discussed earlier.

Aside from plastic surgery, there isn't a lot that we can do about certain physical attributes. But the equation Event + Response = Outcome and Solution applies very well here, too. Unchangeable physical features are merely the events in our lives. They don't need to make or break our experience or our self-esteem. It is our *response* to these features that affects the way we feel. For the changeable aspects of our being—physical or otherwise—again, the power is in our response. We can respond by actively working to improve our appearance, we can resist what is by complaining and putting ourselves down, or we can accept ourselves just the way we are. Your choice all depends on the outcome you want to create in your life.

> 🔲 **Practice the mirror exercise, looking for and acknowledging the qualities that you like about your body. Then, after appreciating what you like about yourself, turn to the parts that you don't like and acknowledge them for how they serve you.**

Our society values physical appearance highly. This has gone to such an extreme that we have forgotten our bodies' purposes aside from sexuality. Our bodies serve us in very powerful ways as the tools that move us through life. Rather than simply judging them based on appearance, we would be wise to focus on the other ways they serve us. Breasts, for example, were designed to feed babies. That is their main function. We tend to judge them as too big or too small or too this or that when we look in the mirror, rather than honoring their functionality.

When I stand in front of a mirror, the most difficult parts to love are my thighs. However, if every time I see them, I send them negativity, who's to say that each nasty thought isn't the very thing that turns into cellulite, or worse yet, illness. Instead, I send my thighs appreciation for walking, running, and supporting me in everything I do. Our minds are very powerful, so I prefer to send my body love and support to affirm its strength and wellness, rather than unhappiness and disgust. Also, if I choose to love my body, I am far more likely to treat it properly with healthy food and exercise. If nothing else, sending these acknowledgements makes me feel better about myself, which is a more attractive way to show up in the world.

> ▦ **Conscientiously be kind to your body until it becomes habitual. Doing this, you will create a strength and confidence when meeting new people that will shine from within and will be seen by others.**

Don't Take It Personally

When we put our picture online, we not only open ourselves up to attracting others, we also open ourselves up to their criticism. While you and I may realize relationships are more than skin deep, not everyone plays by this rule online. Several people complained to me that, regardless of the fact that they are completely honest about their bodies' shape, size, or looks, people are still rude and hurtful. Says Jennifer, "After seeing my profile, where it clearly states that I am overweight or have a few extra pounds, guys will ask for a body picture and then say, 'Sorry, I don't like fat women.'" Whether you're online or off, there is *never* an excuse for being rude.

When someone treats you poorly or says something mean, the E + R = OS equation can help you to handle your emotions. *When someone says something mean, it reveals more about them than it does about you.* If it is truthful and mean, they aren't telling you anything you don't already know about yourself, but they are educating you about their own disposition. *How you respond to what they say is what is revealing about you.* At times like this, your personal code of ethics will help you to determine your best response—and will illuminate for you why that person's words are not worth a second thought.

Jennifer explained, "My initial reaction to the guy who said he didn't like fat women was to be crushed. After I thought about it for a while, I realized that his comment was about *him,* not me. I could choose to be overweight and angry, or overweight and at peace with myself. I merely replied, "Thank you for sharing. I will continue my search for a man with more depth, while you continue your search for a woman with less." A sense of humor about all of this is priceless.

> **If you encounter unkind words from people online, consider carefully who you really are and choose thoughts, words, and feelings that are in alignment with that knowledge as your response.**

7

The Virtual You

I REMEMBER CLEARLY feeling sick to my stomach on the way to my first radio interview. I thought that I had the flu or was fighting off some sort of illness, when my friend suggested that perhaps I was simply nervous. At first, I thought he was being ridiculous; I had spoken to thousands of people before and am comfortable with public speaking. However, the more I thought about it, the more I realized that it was true—I really was nervous. On the radio it would be different; I wouldn't have the benefit of eye contact or my smile to help me "win over" the audience. Until that moment I hadn't realized how much I depended on my physical self to portray to people that I am a good, kind person. Without it, I felt I would be judged on a whole different scale, and I didn't know if I would pass the test.

So, who are you without your winning smile or killer hairdo? Now that you've considered what visual images to display online, it's time to develop the words and language that represent the rest of you. Presenting yourself in this way is an interesting exercise. There is so much that we need to convey to a potential partner, but where do we begin? This chapter will guide you to explore and share the most important aspects of your real self in your virtual presentation. The clarity you gain will be useful for filling out profile questionnaires and engaging in interesting conversations with potential partners. As you work through the self-exploration exercises in this chapter, write your discoveries in your journal or notebook. Begin by considering the following questions:

- **How do you describe yourself—aside from your physical attributes?**

- **What is it about you that you most want someone to know?**

Creating an Imaginary Website— All about You

Recently, as I was developing a website to feature my work as a speaker and author, I became acutely aware that, unlike other sites that sell goods and services, my site's main product was essentially *me!* This raised a number of questions. I had to consider, in depth, what I wanted the site to say about me, who I wanted to attract to my services (i.e., my ideal audience), which keywords would direct people to me, what my domain name should be, which pictures I should use, and what organizations and businesses I wanted to be associated with via referring links.

As I worked through these questions, I realized that this was a great exercise in self-awareness—and perfect for those dating online, who are faced with many of the same considerations. In this chapter I'm going to walk you through the steps of developing an imaginary website that is all about you. You don't need to develop a website when dating online, but the thought processes involved in these exercises will provide you with insights, images, and words with which to share yourself in your profile questionnaire and online communications. Who knows, someday you may even decide to use the information to create a real website. Many people are now creating sites that are dedicated to advertising themselves as single, describing their lives and interests in more depth than is possible in a short dating-service profile.

▨ **As you answer the questions in each of the following sections, pretend that you are creating a personal website in which you are the product, and record your answers.**

Who Do You Want to Attract?

This question requires slightly different considerations when you are looking at attracting people to a business versus your personal life, but many of the values issues remain the same. I wanted people who were interested in personal, spiritual, or business growth to find my site. I also wanted to attract people who cared about creating healthy relationships, whether in the workplace, the home, or the heart.

Most of us have at least a vague sense of the qualities or the kind of people we want to attract in terms of potential romantic partners. I say "vague" because, until we are asked to state our preferences or requirements in our online profile, most of us have never taken the time to really think through and *write down* what we want in a partner, and to state very clearly what we *don't* want. We are rarely conscious and explicit about the nonnegotiable qualities we require in a partnership. Nonnegotiable issues are those that are so important to us that we are unwilling or unable to compromise on them without sacrificing something of ourselves.

Nonnegotiable issues spring from our core values and goals. For instance, if you are absolutely certain that you want to have children, finding someone who also wants children and who has parenting qualities that you respect is a nonnegotiable item. As you probe deeper you may find that hidden within your parenting requirement are some additional, parenting-related requirements—kindness, respectfulness, consistency, fairness, an even temper—you get the picture. For many people, religion or spirituality is a nonnegotiable item. In determining your nonnegotiables, be sure to also include those that you are *not* willing to have in your life, such as substance abuse, physical abuse, or dishonesty.

◈ **Think about the qualities that you want a life partner to have and those that you are not willing to accept in your life. Which qualities are nonnegotable? Which are desirable? Which ones are nice to have? Do you strive to embody those qualities yourself?**

Which Photographs Would You Use?

In Chapter 6 we discussed how to use profile photographs, but in this exercise you are not limited by any of the same constraints. Since this chapter is about self-exploration, the photos you choose in this exercise will be posted only in your *imaginary* website—unless you decide to go on to develop a real one.

Think of several pictures that represent you, recognizing that you don't need to be concerned with scanners, cameras, or whether anyone will see the actual photographs. You can even choose pictures that have never been taken. Selecting these images is an exercise in recognizing what you value and what you wish to portray about yourself. By taking the time to think this through, you can come up with words to describe in your profile the essence, or values, that these photos would convey about you.

For my imaginary website, I would choose two pictures from my youth—one in which I'm being held by my mom and another in which I'm cuddling with my dad by the fireplace. These two memories are favorites and represent several aspects of my personality. I have a very close relationship with my parents and my family is important to me. I have a childlike enthusiasm, and cherish cuddling with the people I love. Along with these childhood pictures, I would show the rest of my family and my husband, Steve, along with our cat and dog, because they all mean so much to me. I would include a picture of me scuba diving or by a waterfall, as I am happiest when in the arms of Mother Nature. I would also post a picture of me teaching, as a huge focus in my life is service through my career. So the themes of love, nature, service, and career emerge as I consider and select my representative photographs for my imaginary website.

As you can see, the actual photographs aren't really necessary to paint a picture that reveals important aspects of one's personality. When you are posting your profile or communicating via e-mail, use words to describe the themes that emerge from the chosen photos in your imaginary website. These themes represent your values.

> ▦ **Which pictures would you choose to represent your life and why? Remember to choose pictures that are in alignment with what you want to attract. Use what you discover about yourself here to help you present yourself better online— and off.**

In terms of finding a mate, we often want a person who is a certain way—active, friendly, healthy—but forget that it helps if we are that way ourselves. Expecting more from someone else than we are willing to offer isn't fair. Look into your personal photo album for the evidence that you are what you say you are and that you are what you want to attract. If you aren't, set about making changes in your life to bring about this alignment.

What Would Your Domain Name Be?

Every aspect of what you put online is information about you, from your listed member name to your photograph, to all the words you use to describe yourself. When designing my professional website, I struggled with the ideal domain name for it. I had a hard time deciding whether the site should be about me (www.EveHogan.com) or what I teach (www.HeartPath.com). I ended up creating two sites, instead of one, each with a slightly different focus.

> ▦ **What would you name your website? What does this name reveal about you?**

Distilling your essence into a few meaningful words is a challenging, yet valuable, task. Our choice of a name is very revealing—whether for our virtual domain or our anonymous username or "handle." When I asked participants in a workshop what their domain name would be, I enjoyed listening to their on-the-spot responses. (If these are actual websites, it is strictly a coincidence.) One woman said hers would be "HotBabe.com." You can easily imagine the kind of attention her website would attract!

Some responses were more introspective. A 30-year-old man shared, "Mine would be BlueSquall.com, because I love the ocean and most times I can be calm, yet there is a side of me that just likes to open up and raise a little bit of hell once in a while." Another man in his 20s said his would be "GreatGuy.com, because I have all the qualities to be a wonderful boyfriend to any woman." A woman in her 40s replied with Intelligent.com, obviously revealing what she values, while a woman in her 20s claimed www.supermom.com, going on to explain she is the single mother of three kids under 5! The range of domains chosen was vast.

Something as simple as a domain name can reveal either qualities that someone is looking for or the kind of person they are likely to attract. The same is true of online membership names and e-mail addresses. Your chosen username is your anonymous identity online, and the first impression you will give others. If you are looking for a long-term, meaningful relationship, having a name with a sexual innuendo may attract men or women for different reasons than your charm, intelligence, and great parenting skills. I've had people write to me with name handles such as LadiesMan or SexyBabe, who claim to be suprised that they cannot find monogamy and lasting love online. These folks have a big discrepancy between how they are presenting themselves and what they desire in a relationship.

One man in his 40s explained that he had to change his handle because he was getting such a negative response. He had been a CB radio operator for 25 years, so when he signed onto the Web he used his old radio handle, NightStalker, only to be told repeatedly by the women online that he sounded like an axe murderer. Needless to say, he changed his name quickly, recognizing that what works in one realm of communication does not necessarily transfer to another.

On the other side of the spectrum, a man in his late 20s chose the name Klipspringer, which was very meaningful to him, although I'd be surprised if many others were familiar with it. He explains, "A Klipspringer antelope is known for mating with its partner for life. I consider myself to be monogamous and a relationship person. If someone were to take the time to look up what a Klipspringer is, they might learn something about me. In addition, I would know they value education by wanting to learn something new."

Your name is often the first thing people will see when deciding who to contact or whose profile to read. While coming up with something cute, clever, descriptive, original, *and in alignment with your goals* may be challenging, the effort is worth it. Your chosen name can pull people in or push them away, so think about what you really want to say about yourself when you sign on. A great way to begin a conversation with someone online is to ask them what their chosen username means to them.

What usernames do you currently use online? What do they say about you?

You will also learn about yourself by paying attention to the usernames to which you are drawn as you browse dating sites. For example, I logged on to one free online dating service and did a search by a certain geographic criterion. My search returned a list of usernames from which I could click through to the members' profiles. A sampling of some of the names that appeared were: Absolute Angel, Affinity Seeker, Alley Cat, All Heart, Big, Bigheart4U, Blkman4U2use, Good Catch, Guilt Trips, Shy Guy, 2Hot2Handle, and 69. If I were genuinely looking for a relationship, I would be drawn to names like All Heart, Good Catch, or Affinity Seeker. Out of curiosity, I might read profiles under names like Guilt Trips or 2Hot2Handle, but in search of a suitable partner, I would never seriously consider a person who labeled himself that way. If you are self-observant, something about your own values will be revealed to you by the names you choose to look at further.

🔲 **Everything is information. Pay attention!**

A 49-year-old man shared this interesting observation: "I think people get what they *look for,* not what they want. If you want quiet and loving but you look for stylish, flashy, and shallow, guess what you are going to get!" His point is well made.

As you engage in online dating, be aware if you begin to find a mismatch between what you want and what you are getting. Look back for clues that you were offered in the beginning. Did you choose someone because their picture showed them in front of an expensive car, when what you were looking for was someone with a kind heart? Did you choose them because of the sexuality they promised in their words, when what you were looking for was someone who had the same values as you?

What Are Your Keywords?

Now that you have named your personal website, consider which keywords represent you. Keywords are the words that search engines use to list sites in their search results and lead people to those sites. Just like your name, your keywords are very revealing about who you are and what you value. For example, for my professional site the keywords I chose included "responsibility, relationships, personal growth, spirituality, intellectual foreplay, virtual foreplay, dating tips, self-esteem," and "love." These words reflect my work, and they also reflect quite a bit about me personally.

▨ **Consider all the things that are important to you—personality characteristics, activities, and hobbies—and list up to twenty-five words that best describe you. Remember, these are the words that could lead your life mate to you, so be sure that they are reflective of your body, mind, and spirit!**

One 24-year-old man participating in this exercise realized how personal themes had begun to emerge in his answers to these questions. As well as a face shot, he included a photo on his site that showed him horseback riding. For his domain name he chose www.horseman.com. His keywords were "horses, riding, friendly, caring, outdoors, countryside, fun." He then added playfully, "I like horses—are you noticing that trend?"

A few people complained to me that everyone on the Internet was looking for the same qualities in a person or portraying the same qualities in themselves as everyone else, making distinguishing one person from another difficult. This could be in part because of the nature of the online questionnaire that they were filling out. Some sites only offer multiple-choice options, leaving people with answers that all sound the same. Multiple-choice options make the questions simpler for people to answer and make it easier for the computer to sort matches for you. Unfortunately, this leaves little room for creativity and individuality to emerge. *This is where your responsibility comes in.* If an online dating service offers you a space for essay questions, let your creativity shine through in your answers. Give more, not less, of yourself. If you are still at a loss for what to say, draw from this exercise and share your keywords. The same holds true when you want to draw out information from someone else. You may be pleasantly surprised by the results if you ask someone what *their* keywords would be.

> ▣ **When reading other people's keywords, pay attention to subtleties—the order in which they list their words, the combinations of words they choose, even the repetition of words that mean the same thing. You may discover interesting themes. Can you see your own themes emerging?**

Carl, a man in his 30s, listed his keywords as: "intelligent, creative, artistic, active, enthusiastic, vocal, lively," and "relaxed." His repetitive use of "creative" and "artistic" adds an extra emphasis to these qualities and reveals their importance to him. A man in his 20s, Tom, said his words were: "single, bachelor, handsome, responsible, secure, intelligent, thoughtful, caring, sexy, morals."

Some interesting things emerge in Tom's keywords that merit further exploration. First, he listed both "single" and "bachelor," which mean the same thing and emphasize his availability. After several attractive qualities, he added "sexy" toward the *end* of his list. He wanted his being sexy included as a nice quality, and, if I were looking at him as a potential mate, I'd appreciate that this wasn't the first thing on his mind. I would also value that he immediately followed "sexy" with "morals." I also like that he included a little bit about his looks, his sense of security, and how he treats others. Notice that *what I pay attention to* about what someone else says reveals as much information about me and my values as it does about him—if not more! *The same is true for you.*

> ▣ **Pay attention to what captures your attention in someone else's profile or e-mails. Information about your own values will be revealed in what matters to you most in someone else.**

Danny chose the following keywords: "Mr. Right, Mr. Mom, Most Eligible Bachelor," and "Good Guy." Here he implicitly lets us know that he has kids, is available, and considers himself to be a good person. Cynthia, a woman in her 30s, used the following keywords: "honest, recovering person, nonsmoker, communication, sense of humor, commitment, reading, swimming, dancing, movies, music, single mom." While she sounds kind and sincere, the words "recovering person" right at the beginning leave a lot of room for interpretation—recovering from what? Is she recovering from something emotional or physical, and how far along she is in the healing process. What draws *your* attention in the words that she listed? Asking questions of someone that reflect your curiosity or shared interests is a great launching pad for a conversation.

Everything is information—even a lack of information. Trina, a woman in her 30s, said that her keywords would be: "single woman, dating channel, love on the Web, eligible bachelorettes," and "women seeking men." All we are really clear about is that Trina is looking for a man and she is very available. Lana, a 31-year-old woman, said her keywords would be: "natural, sweet, attractive, beautiful, dark, exotic girl, nice." These paint a lovely mental picture of her physical being, but also leave a lot of mystery about her likes and dislikes. This offers a great place to begin asking her questions to fill in the gaps. However, as you fill out your questionnaire surveys, consider that people will gravitate to the profiles that reveal what they want to know.

In response to the keywords question, one man, Ray, offered only "47-year-old male." He listed his domain name as LookingFor ALady.com. If pulling teeth for information is someone's idea of fun, Ray may get a response, but more likely, with his lack of specifics, online dating will prove to be a dead end for him. One thing most of us want in a partner is someone who is interesting and is willing to put some effort into the relationship. Consider this as you fill out the online profiles. Having to pry to get information may cause the person of your dreams to simply click on someone else's profile.

Take your time and be sure your profile reflects the most important aspects of your being.

What Are Your Links?

Many websites have links that connect to related sites or sites that are endorsed by the one you logged on to. When I had my first professional website designed, the Webmaster included links without discussing them with me. When I logged on to the site for the first time, I found links to a housecleaning service (which was probably more appropriate than I realized!) and other local businesses that had nothing to do with my work. This prompted me to consider what my criteria for links from my site would be. These links should reflect my values and be useful to my clients.

For this exercise, my personal website would include links to www.MauiUnderwater.com, because I love to scuba dive, and to spiritual organizations and resources such as www.Vedanta.org and www.GraceCathedral.org. I would add a link to my publisher's website, www.hunterhouse.com, since it has been such an instrumental part of my life and its books are great resources. I would also link to www.VoiceAVision.com, where people can post their vision for a project or a dream they want to create and find other people who want to help. This idea really excites me—and is a glimmer of what I talk about more in Chapter 14, "Making the Net Work."

> **Which associations, businesses, or organizations would you link to from your site as an indicator of your interests? Are there products, people, or places with which you feel an alliance? Carefully consider these questions and list your personal links. What do your links say about you?**

Deciding on the links for your imaginary website doesn't require research into actual sites. Just consider the activities, businesses, people, places, or products that are important to you. Our associations provide information about what kind of people we are. By identifying your links, you will deepen the process of self-discovery and expression. Ask the people you are meeting online about their associations, since that might work well as a launching pad for revealing conversations.

Lily, a woman whose domain name would be www.YourPartnerLoverFriend.com, said her keywords would be: "honest, loving, sensual, active, intelligent, sexy, happy, and high energy." When I asked about her links, she said, "companies that are trustworthy and have great products; people that offer value to others." This answer reveals information about what Lily finds important. Now, the question to be explored is whether or not she lives in alignment with what she says matters to her.

A man in his 20s claimed he would have links to "support groups—nonprofit and educational: Save the Children, battered women, eating disorders, relationship building." The first question I would ask him is whether his interest in these is personal or more of a social concern. This would likely begin an interesting conversation.

Another young man in his 20s stated that he would link to "the Boy Scouts and U.S. Marines. I am a proud member of them both." I immediately imagine that he likes (or needs) structure and that giving service is a value of his. The first thing I might ask him would be what he likes most about both of these alliances. A woman in her late 40s said, "My links would be to bookstores, education, and beauty. These things belong in my life." Her links made me feel an immediate sense of commonality. Ed, a man in his 40s, revealed a lot about himself when he said, "There would be no links on my site. I don't want anyone leaving it."

The challenge in all of this is, of course, that there is a lot of room for us to fill in the blanks about other people, making assumptions that may not be correct. The solution is to check out your assumptions for accuracy by asking lots of questions—and listening to the answers.

Mixed Messages

As you develop the virtual you, can you see your personality shining through in your online persona? Are your values identifiable in your virtual presentation? Hopefully, you are becoming skilled at recognizing themes as they emerge and using that information to further explore online communication. Now let's practice guessing where a person is coming from based on their personal website metaphors.

Donald, a 26-year-old, listed his keywords as "absent-minded smart-ass, big, lovable, teddy bear, friendly, open-minded, huggable, caring." The domain name he chose was www.AbsentMinded-SmartAss.com, because, "that is what I am." I don't know about you, but I immediately receive mixed messages from this. "Absent-minded" and "caring" don't go well together, nor do "smart-ass" and "friendly." Ironically, Donald has used several keywords that are attractive, but he chose not to feature them in his domain name. It's not surprising that Donald went on to say that he has received no response from online dating, and sadly, when asked what he had learned about himself, he replied, "no one loves me." There are so many more *empowering* things that Donald could learn about himself from online dating if he just practiced self-observation. Donald needs to take a look at his own contradictory characteristics and begin the work to align who he is, what matters to him, and what he wants with what he is sharing with the world.

Here is another interesting situation. What would you think about a 37-year-old woman who chose her member name, LacyNight, "because it is sexy"? Her keywords are "alluring, sexy, attractive, erotic, wild," and "daring." She would link her personal site to "lacy underwear and sexy lingerie sites" and her domain name would be SexyPlusSeductive.com. While a lot is left unsaid about her interests and values, there is not much mystery about the kind of response she is going to get! Ironically, when asked about cyber sex, she answered, "I usually don't do that and I think it is rude for a man to assume that women do that right off the bat."

Throughout the development of your imaginary website, and in your actual profiles and correspondences with others, beware of mixed messages. In order to turn your online relationships into real-life successes, be sure to align your words with what you want to create.

▩ **Look carefully at the messages you are sending the world. If you are receiving a certain response from people over and over again, before you blame them for being rude, disrespectful, or uninterested, evaluate the message you are giving in your words, profile, picture, and membership name. If all these are in order you can point fingers, but not before then. Remember, too, that your power is in how you respond to events.**

PART THREE

Making Contact

"I learned that words and communication are probably the most important part of a relationship to me. I never realized that before. What I have chosen in former relationships was based on someone's physical being."

JANET, 50s

"I can easily write things I would never find myself actually saying to someone on a date, for instance. I find that people tend to get really personal in a way they never would if they had just met me and we dated."

ALFREDO, 44

"I can weed out liars from the sincere people fairly quickly now. A few well-placed questions can let me know right away what quality of person I am dealing with on the other end."

NANCY, 43

"I think anything goes online and no one is afraid to ask. Everyone has guts online."

CAROLYN, 36

8

Practicing Intellectual Foreplay Online

"Chose your life's mate carefully. From this one decision will come 90 percent of all your happiness or misery."
— H. JACKSON BROWN, JR., *LIFE'S LITTLE INSTRUCTION BOOK*

L ET'S TAKE A LOOK AT WHERE WE ARE in this process. You've already established your own code of ethics to guide your behavior while dating online. You've identified several of your personal values, your nonnegotiable issues, and what you have to offer. You've uncovered the importance of self-observation and making choices in alignment with your goals. You've looked at yourself pretty closely—now let's take a look at who you want in your life and how to make effective contact.

As I was researching my book *Intellectual Foreplay: Questions for Lovers and Lovers-to-Be,* it became obvious that many people get into relationships simply on the basis of "looks good" and "feels good," only to find themselves in a situation that truly *is not* good. People actually ask more questions about a car they are buying than they do about a potential partner or life mate. Consequently, we find ourselves in physically intimate relationships with people we know no better than a stranger. By contrast, the Internet has emerged as a place where people are asking questions and sharing intimate information with others they wouldn't recognize if they passed on the street.

In *Intellectual Foreplay*, I encourage people to explore intellectual, emotional, spiritual, and physical compatibility by asking questions and listening to the answers. My goal is for people to use their *heads,* as well as their hearts, in choosing their life mate. The challenge for many folks offline is that, once they are attracted to each other physically, it is much harder to pay attention to the warning signs that indicate there isn't a match on critical issues. Stopping a relationship midstream can be difficult when it looks and feels good—even when you know that ultimately it isn't good. Unfortunately, when big issues are ignored, they emerge later in a more painful and complicated manner.

The challenge for people meeting online is the exact opposite of the challenge for those who meet in person. People are much better at letting go of an online relationship than a face-to-face one when their core values or nonnegotiable issues are not in alignment. If someone says something strange online or mentions an interest that their date doesn't share, they may simply never receive a reply again. The sheer volume of options online causes people to more readily screen out potential mismatches. People who meet in person tend to stay in relationships that they know aren't good for them, while people who have only met online tend to dismiss potential relationships that may even have worked out well had they been able to meet in person.

> **Consider how this has been for you. Have you stayed in face-to-face relationships longer than you felt you should have? Have you dismissed people online more quickly? Pay attention to the criteria for a good partner that emerge when you evaluate your actions.**

Balance, Intuition, and Risk Taking

Choosing whom to date online requires balance, risk taking, and intuition. We would do well to balance the ease of letting go of relationships on the Net with our generous tendency to give people a chance. Somewhere in between is the perfect balance. If you analyze a relationship too much, you will never get married, but if you don't ask enough questions or pay enough attention, you will surely get divorced. Sometimes you simply have to trust your gut instinct—giving someone you might not normally consider a chance or dropping someone who appears okay because you have an uncomfortable feeling about them.

Carol, a 31-year-old woman, told me this story: "I responded to an e-mail from a man although I originally wasn't going to. I already had a lot of e-mail pen pals and wasn't looking for any more. But Rick lived an hour and a half away, and a particular phrase he used struck me as humorous, so I complimented him on it. He wrote back and we managed to meet up in an instant chat. We chatted for a couple of nights, then he hopped in his car to drive out to visit me. Since we had both been honest from the start, it was wonderful to have our initial attraction to each other confirmed. We are now seeing each other regularly, taking turns with the commute." It's just as simple as that: if Carol hadn't written on impulse, or instinct, they would have never met and their relationship would have never happened.

John, a man in his 40s, agreed: "You may be writing somebody who's actually a really great person, maybe even a soul mate, and due to the fact that you can't really know someone solely by writing, you may just let them go. Whereas, if you'd met in person, you might be motivated to continue to work on getting to know them."

On the other hand, Linda, a 28-year-old woman, said, "I have learned to trust my instincts online. Once a man expressed a desire to get to know me better, so I read his profile again and I got the heebie-jeebies. It was strange. I was just certain something was wrong. I sent a note saying, 'thanks, but no thanks.' Then, I kept thinking about how that feeling came across so clearly, so I went back to read his profile again to see what had turned me off, but there was nothing strange or odd. I just got a bad feeling and trusted it."

To find your match, you will have to take some risks. You have to make contact, you have to ask questions, you have to share your thoughts and feelings, you have to spend some time, and at some point, you're going to have to meet in person. All the while, paying attention to your intuition and watching for any warning signs is a wise thing to do. More on how to meet safely will be discussed in Chapter 12, "Close Encounters."

As you know, when I met my husband, Steven, he was having dinner alone in a restaurant. My intuition spurred me to talk to him. I watched him for a while, but he wasn't paying much attention to me. I could easily have figured that he was not available or dating the waitress or just not interested, but the way I saw it, I had nothing to lose. I hadn't had a relationship with him before that moment, so in the worst-case scenario, if he turned me down, nothing would have changed. As it turned out, we're happily together almost a decade later because I took the risk and followed my intuition.

> ▨ **As you read other people's profiles and receive responses to your own, pay attention to what causes you to dismiss someone's advances or bypass their profile listing. Are you reacting to something they said or a gut feeling? Do you find that you handle these choices differently online than you do in person? Remember to self-observe—by doing so you'll be able to consciously develop and access your decision-making skills.**

Love Requirements: Must Be Able to Type, Spelling Is a Must

While, for the most part, we all seek certain similar qualities in a partner, lifestyles, goals, and interests vary significantly. Online, we must become our own matchmaker, taking an active role in figuring out who is a potential partner and whether we have a foundation on which to build a solid relationship.

People can have some pretty funny differences in what they are looking for in a relationship, which is why *it pays to ask*. Lydia told me, "I met this guy on the Internet who was asking me a bunch of unusual questions. Apparently the woman whom he had met just prior to me turned out to be a lesbian looking for a sperm donor. When he told her he'd been fixed, that pretty much ended their lunch date!" Another woman in her 50s said, "I had to tell one individual that I thought we had too many different interests to find a mutual ground to get to know each other. After all, I have never had a desire to ride naked on the back of a Harley, and I doubt that he would enjoy wearing a tux to the ballet."

One 43-year-old woman shared her particular set of challenges. "A lot of men want thin women. I explain up front that I am full-figured and then send them my photos. Those who continue to talk to me know what I look like, which narrows the field considerably. I also do not narrow my vocabulary and generally check my spelling. I belong to Mensa (a club for people with genius IQ levels) and need to find someone who can accept me for who I am—a smart, fat chick with five cats!" I'm sure she'd be pleased to know that Timothy Leary said, "Intelligence is the ultimate aphrodisiac!"

As I mentioned already, there are huge numbers of senior citizens using the Internet as a means of making contact—for finding friends and potential sweethearts. Several of them told me that their requirements for a partner have changed as they have matured. One woman said, "At this age, I have found my matches to be more laid back and tolerant of things that younger men might not be. Younger people are more concerned with the physical than older people." Since many people at this age have already had families and careers, their requirements for a partner also reflect a different set of circumstances.

While it is necessary that we have a clear picture of what we want and don't want in relationships, we also have to get clear on what is *really* important and what isn't. Sometimes, over-stringent requirements become barriers keeping love out, instead of filters for letting love in. If everyone is looking for perfection, but no one is advertising it, we are all destined for loneliness. By the same token, quite often by pointing our fingers at the other person (the event), we are avoiding looking at ourselves and taking responsibility.

In front of her 8-year-old son, Carla lamented with a heavy sigh, "Everyone in the profiles says they are looking for the same things. Their profiles are full of clichés—candlelight dinners, walks on the beach—and the men are all looking for someone 'equally comfortable in jeans or an evening gown.'" She ended, "Nine out of ten of them say that!" at which point her son chirped, *"Well then, find the one who doesn't!"*

This innocent 8-year-old makes a very good point—make it your task to find the one out of ten with whom you are in true alignment! Not only are there millions of people online, but those millions of people are real people who live in the real world. They could be your neighbors, coworkers, the guy in the restaurant, or the girl who just smiled at you. Single people who want partners abound. Your job is to find the ones who have the qualities you are looking for *and to be a partner worthy of finding yourself!*

Consider what you would do if you needed a job. Undoubtedly, you would do some research, reading want ads online or in the newspaper, and you'd send out inquiries asking questions about available jobs. If a job promised what you were looking for, and you had the appropriate skills, you'd arrange for an interview, make yourself presentable, and show up a little early in order to make a good impression. In the interview, you'd exchange questions to establish further compatibility and pay attention to the qualities of your potential coworkers. After the interview, if you were still interested, you would follow up. You might even have to follow up several times or participate in multiple interviews. If you didn't get the job, would you give up? Of course not! You'd keep looking until you found the right job for you.

Online dating is a similar process. Reading profiles is like sorting through the want ads to determine which person intrigues you; has the qualities, lifestyle, and assets that you are looking for; and is looking for the things you have to offer. Now, you need to send out the inquiry and see if you are compatible, and, if so, arrange a face-to-face meeting.

> ▨ **Do your homework. Be proactive. Spend some time scanning the profiles and choosing the lucky people you want to send an e-mail to as an introduction of yourself.**

Ask, Ask, Ask

Practicing intellectual foreplay online begins with clarifying what is important to you and then asking a potential partner pertinent questions to help you see if you two are a match. Many of the basic questions that you would ask someone upon meeting—marital status, age, religion, and so on—may already be answered in their profile, but feel free to ask again, just for clarity's sake. Sometimes a profile can be a few years old and certain dynamics may have changed.

My previous book *Intellectual Foreplay* contains hundreds of questions to guide you in knowing what to ask a potential partner. This applies not only to online interactions, but also to the initial stages of dating face-to-face. Do you dread first dates because you don't know what to talk about? In *Intellectual Foreplay* you will find questions on just about every topic, including entertainment, education, past experiences, future goals, spiritual beliefs, commitment, children, and sex, to name a few. An excellent way to start conversations is to ask questions based on your own values and nonnegotiable issues. Refer to the exercise in the last chapter in which you identified your nonnegotiable issues and use them as a guide for doing the following exercise.

> ▨ **What do you need to ask someone before you get seriously involved? Begin by making a list of your top twenty questions.**

As you ask questions of your potential partners, it is important to note that *there are no right or wrong answers.* There are answers that are in alignment with what you are looking for and answers that are not. No one likes to be asked questions when they think they are being judged. Job interviews are uncomfortable because we feel the pressure to have the "right" answer to be hired. While there are some similarities between online dating and job hunting, no one enjoys a "love interview" either, and a budding relationship doesn't need that kind of discomfort. Approach the process of engaging your e-dates in intellectual foreplay naturally and playfully. This is the wonderful and stimulating process of getting to know someone— so enjoy!

On the next page two pages are a few questions taken from *Intellectual Foreplay* to help you get started. Even more important than asking someone else these questions is answering them yourself. As you explore your own beliefs in each of these different realms, you will gain insight into what matters to you. You will then be in a better position to generate the questions that you want to explore with someone else. In order to discover a match, you have to know what you are *matching with*—which is where your own answers come into play.

Questions to Engage Your Date in Intellectual Foreplay

* What do you like about yourself? What would you like to improve?
* What do you want out of a relationship now?
* What qualities do you find attractive in another person?
* What do you like to do for fun?
* What has your favorite age or time period been in your life so far? Why?

* How well do you communicate—in writing, verbally, physically, and telepathically?
* How do you typically use your time?
* What are your spiritual beliefs?
* What are your values and how do you prioritize them?
* What does romance mean to you and how important is it?
* How do you see yourself in the future? What are your goals?
* What is your educational background or future goal?
* What is your relationship with your family?
* Who are your closest friends and why?
* How do you see yourself financially?
* How is your health and how do you maintain or improve it?
* What is your occupation and how do you feel about it?
* What habits do you have that you like and don't like?
* Describe your eating peculiarities and preferences.
* What are your preferences for the ideal home and climate?
* Describe your ideal vacation.
* What are your favorite holidays and how do you spend them?
* What are your feelings and expectations about having and raising children?
* Describe the best wedding you ever went to and what you liked about it.
* How comfortable or willing are you to talk about sex?

Whether you are communicating online, over the phone, or in person, being prepared with questions for exploration will serve you well. How you go about asking the questions depends on your personal style. Rita explains that immediately after someone contacts her via e-mail, she begins asking her top twenty questions. She has them organized in order of priority, with her nonnegotiable issues at the top. Rather than overwhelm someone with all twenty at once, she includes one or two questions—and her own answers—in each e-mail. "My feeling is that if we discuss my first ten questions and we are still e-mailing, then I'm willing to meet them. We can discuss the rest in person."

Gary's style is a little more subtle. "I like to look over my questions when I am alone, consider what really matters to me, and then I just weave the topic into the conversation on a date or into an e-mail. It is amazing what people will tell you if you simply bother to ask." Tanya says her approach is to simply say, "I have this great book full of questions, let's practice a little *intellectual foreplay* and see where it leads!" She adds with a smile, "No one has turned me down yet!"

> **What is your conversational style: casual, formal, serious, humorous, or to the point?**

Listen, Listen, Listen

Another great way of generating questions is to review someone's profile and ask them questions about interests or things that they have stated. This approach has multiple benefits: it gives you a great launching point for conversation, lets the other person feel heard and appreciated, and establishes that you might have common ground. Susan says, "I love it when a man repeats back to me what I said in my profile that intrigued him." There is nothing like having someone say, "I loved your comment about the night sky and that caused me to write to you. I, too, love to gaze at the stars."

Susan goes on to add, "On the other hand, I can't stand it when someone just writes to me because of my picture, completely ignoring my preferences, and not commenting on anything that I wrote." Louise is also looking for more meaningful initial contact: "I posted my profile on a site and the very next day I got an e-mail. Excited, I opened it. The man just introduced himself and said, 'I am very interested in you.' It was nice, but so impersonal. I wanted to know *why* he was interested in me—and why I should be interested in him, too."

Pay attention to what people say in their profiles, e-mails, and conversations. Honor their preferences, ask questions, and *interact with them*. Practicing this kind of intellectual foreplay conveys that you are paying attention and want to know more. It will help you identify people who have real potential and take you further down the path of making informed, value-based decisions about your e-dates.

> 🔲 **Pay attention to what makes you curious and use it as a launching pad for practicing intellectual foreplay and active listening in your e-mail interactions. Then, transfer those skills to your face-to-face conversations.**

Alignment of Words and Actions

Of course, you'll want to take in more information than simply how someone answers your questions. This is a little trickier online than in person, because for the most part all you have to go on are their words. However, how quickly someone responds and whether they do what they say they will do can be determined to a certain extent via e-mail and chats. This is similar to what we discussed about people's keywords; if you pay attention, you will see themes emerge in what people say and in their actions. Themes are actually even easier to see when people are writing because you can go back, reread their words, and really consider what was said.

One of my college professors, Dr. Larry Iannaccone, used to say to his students, "Social structure leaves its finger prints on everything it touches." He went on to explain that if you listen carefully to the words people use repeatedly and the topics they bring up, themes will emerge that reveal what the person's social structure is, what their belief systems are—essentially, how they think. You can take this analysis even further by paying attention to where they hang out, who their friends are, what kind of books they read, and so forth. *Everything is information;* you just have to pay attention! (Are you beginning to see a theme in this book?)

Ironically, people will often tell you right at the beginning of a relationship exactly what the problem will be. They may write to say, "I know that the distance is going to be a problem, *but…*" and off you go, into a relationship in which the distance will be the problem. They may say, "I am probably too old for you, *but…*" or "I don't have any money, *but…*" or "I don't want kids, *but….*" Those can be really big "buts"! Pay attention to your own use of "but" as well. "But" tends to cancel out whatever came before it. When you say or hear, "I love you, but…" know that whatever is said after that little three-letter word will take away the power of the three-word phrase that came before it. Watch out for big "buts"; they signal a conflict within your correspondent and potential conflict in the relationship, should you venture into one.

Oh, What a Tangled Web We Weave…

No matter how many questions you ask, there may still be some people who lie to you. While this can be tricky to assess—both online and in person—one way to begin is to watch for *conflicting* themes or information.

Peter described his experience: "I had exchanged photos and chatted one evening with a woman. The next day she sent me a message saying that she wanted to move from England to live with me—she and her 14-year-old son. I explained that I wanted to get to know her better before having her move thousands of miles, concerned that things might not work out. She agreed. We continued to talk and get to know each other. I went out of town for a week and when I returned, she mentioned moving again, only this time she was alone because her son (who was 14 a few weeks ago) was 20 and joining the army. Suddenly, a flag went up that something wasn't right there."

Have you ever taken a personality quiz or aptitude test? After a while, you start to feel as if you are answering the same questions over and over again, just worded differently. You feel that way because you are! These tests are designed with the philosophy that you won't be able to fake an outcome if you are asked the same question in multiple ways. As an individual, you can use this same strategy if you suspect someone of lying on the Net. Ask them a question more than once, in different ways. Unless they are keeping records of what they have written to you, they will eventually reveal inconsistencies.

If you are having doubts about someone, keep your own code of ethics in mind. Your purpose is not to call the other person names, treat them disrespectfully, or "show them a thing or two." Life is too short for that, and my guess is that you'd rather spend your energy moving forward. Your purpose here is simply to find out whether this person is a good partner for you or not. If honesty is a non-negotiable item for you and you discover that they are lying, a reasonable response is to get out. And, you can do so neatly and politely, with grace, then move on to other opportunities.

While being lied to is a horrible experience, the age-old saying that "two wrongs don't make a right" still applies. Taking it upon ourselves to teach someone a lesson seldom creates the desired result of enlightening them. It draws us down to their level, focuses us on the past, and takes us away from our goals and values for the future.

One woman sent me a lengthy letter detailing an elaborate plan of revenge that she had spent months executing in order to get back at a man who had deceived her online. "I lured him in with a false identity, one that I knew he would take as bait. We e-mailed back and forth, hundreds of e-mails, until I knew he was in love with my alter ego. Then I dropped the bomb on him and stopped writing." She added proudly, "I did to him what he did to me." But where did it get her?

If a real, loving relationship is what you want, don't waste your time practicing your skills of deception—these are not the skills that will serve you when you do meet the right person.

> **Through self-observation, your own social structure will become obvious in your online interactions. Are you aligning your thoughts, words, and actions with your relationship goals?**

If At First You Don't Succeed, Ask, Ask, Again

One of the pitfalls of e-mail is that two-way interaction can easily be avoided. People can write back to you without responding to anything that you originally said or asked them. Chats or instant messages reduce the potential for this to a certain degree, since participants are corresponding in real time, but with these technologies people are often writing at the same time and posting their messages simultaneously, so there are constant interruptions in the flow of thought. This makes it particularly challenging to know when someone is avoiding your comments and questions and when they just haven't seen them.

Withholding information can be a form of deception. As you look for your perfect match and engage e-dates in intellectual foreplay, pay attention to the questions they ignore. I have noticed several times that I will e-mail someone asking specific questions, only to find that they answer one or two and avoid the others. Sometimes this is coincidence; other times it is conscious avoidance.

If information isn't volunteered, you need to ask the questions again. Know yourself. Know what you want. Know what you don't want. Know what you have to offer and share that information. Lisa, a senior online, wrote to say, "This one man sent me poetry and pretty pictures, but every time I asked him about himself, he'd only send a line or two. At first, I was distracted by the romantic images, but after several e-mails that yielded no response to my questions, I stopped writing back." Your role as an online date is not to make the other person "wrong" by pointing out his or her oversight, but to simply ask the questions again and see if they elicit a response. Ultimately, asking questions of a partner will yield a lot of information—even if they don't answer.

The equation **Event** + **R**esponse = **O**utcome and Solution applies to the process of intellectual foreplay too. How your potential partner responds to your questions, both in terms of how willing they are to share themselves and what they say, is the event; it is *their* responsibility. What you experience as a result of their words—your thoughts, feelings, and assumptions—and how you choose to respond are *your* responsibility.

Good to You vs. Good for You

In a radio interview I did with him, Nick Lawrence of "Straight Talk" brought up a really interesting question. He asked me about the difference between choosing a partner who is good *for* you versus someone who is good *to* you. If you think about this distinction, you'll see the point he was making. You could be in a relationship with someone who is good *to* you—say, attentive or expressive, sexually satisfying, or sharing the same hobbies—but the nature of the relationship could still not be good *for* you—they might be married or otherwise emotionally unavailable, or they might have conflicting values or lifestyles.

When you consider online relationships, there is a lot of room for this to happen. If you find yourself in a dialog with someone who is interesting and kind to you but is unavailable to meet in person, takes all your time away from your real life, keeps you living in a fantasy world, or draws you into activities or conversations that go against your code of ethics, then the relationship may not be good for you. Only you can make this distinction, but it is critical to keep this in mind. The other person is only an "event"; how you respond to that event is what creates a good or bad outcome for you.

- Think about your past relationships or online communications. Consider the types of people to whom you've been attracted and the interactions that you have had. Pay attention to the kind of men or women you are attracted to as you read through the profiles. Do you tend to be drawn to those who are good to you, good for you, neither, or both?

- If you see a pattern in your own dating behavior that you would like to change, allow online dating to provide you with an opportunity to expand your repertoire of skills and choices. Try something different and see how it works. If you always wait for someone else to initiate contact, try doing so yourself and see what that is like. Stretch!

9

Touched By an E-mail 0:-)

H AVE YOU HEARD ENOUGH about how and why to use your head during online romantic pursuits? Well, don't despair. There are valuable lessons and self-discovery for your heart, too! In this chapter let's examine the subtleties of communicating via e-mail and look at how you can make an innately impersonal technology personal, romantic, and heartwarming.

One woman I met was in the midst of a passionate e-mail affair. She could hardly stand to go out during the day, preferring to stay online in the hopes that her lover would log on and they could chat. There is something so sweet and wonderful about opening your e-mail box and finding a letter from someone who thinks you're special. The power of this is so strong that some people feel intense love and yearning on account of it, or depression and loneliness due to a lack of response. Some race home from work with great anticipation to check their e-mail, while others check their boxes at every opportunity throughout the day.

As you venture into the emotional terrain of Internet courtship, keep in mind the challenges inherent in the written word as a means of intimate communication. On one hand, it encourages our poetic side to emerge in ways that it rarely would if we were speaking face-to-face. People become much more personal in e-mail, revealing aspects of themselves they probably wouldn't share on a date. On the other hand, written communication leaves room for interpretation and reading between the lines, which can lead to misunderstandings if you aren't careful. Nancy, a 33-year-old woman, said that one of the things that she liked about online dating was "having someone's personality in writing." But this can be misleading if people express themselves differently in writing than they do in person.

> ▣ **Pay attention to the person you portray yourself as when you write, and little by little, bring the aspects that you admire about yourself in writing into your daily way of being.**

Jonathan, who is in his 30s, found that he was far more expressive when he wrote to people via e-mail, and it grew to affect other aspects of his life as well. He looked forward to getting on his computer to write. When he stopped to consider how he was different online, he realized that he used e-mail as a sort of journal entry. "When I wrote to women, I would reach into my day, into my heart, and pull out pieces that I would have otherwise missed. My days became more colorful and rich when I knew that I had to pay attention in order to write about it. My life became fuller on account of taking the time to notice what was going on around me and recording it."

I asked Jonathan how he could apply that to his personal relationships off the Net. "A couple of ways come to mind. First, I'm simply more aware now when I am with a date. I notice her jewelry or the shimmer in her hair. Women love it when I comment on the little details that I used to totally miss. Now, when I am with another person—whether my kids or a date—I share what I am seeing and feeling more. I bring more depth to my relationships by doing in person what I have been doing on the Net—sharing more of myself." He smiled and added, "People seem to be really responsive, sharing themselves more, too."

One of the huge benefits of learning the art of elucidating our feelings online is personal awareness and growth. Even with the advantage of being face-to-face with someone, there can be plenty of room for misinterpretation. If we become adept at identifying our emotions and expressing them clearly online, we will become more comfortable sharing our thoughts and feelings with others offline as well. We will be emotionally open to give and to receive more freely.

Think First, Edit, Then Hit "Send"

Professional writers don't submit their very first thoughts for publication. They write a first draft, then reread and rework what they have written to be sure their work captures what they want to say, that it is written in their tone and voice, that it conveys their spirit. If you have aspirations for online courtship, do the same thing with your e-mails. Putting your thoughts in writing involves a much higher level of responsibility than just saying them. Because written words can be read and reread, their effect is amplified. There is no room for denial, but tremendous latitude for misinterpretation. In addition, a unique feature of the Internet is the ease with which your words can be scattered to the universe for anyone to read, beyond your intended recipient. So, "thinking before you speak"—paying attention to what you write—is well worth your time, online or off.

You might be surprised by just how many times I get asked for my opinion about whether an e-mail about to be sent "sounds okay," or what a certain word choice in an e-mail from a suitor "really means." The very nature of e-mail—which lacks tone of voice, inflection, eye messages, smiles, winks, softness, volume, and body language—encourages us to overanalyze the words on the receiving end, grasping for anything that can make the meaning clearer.

As you write to a potential partner, reread your words a few times, wearing several different hats, before you press "send." If you are writing to a total stranger, put on a "safety patrol" hat and screen what you have written to make sure you don't reveal too much too soon. Then, read your e-mail as if you were a stranger, to see if, from that perspective, you have said anything that can be misconstrued.

I have a male friend, Dennis, whom I met on the Internet and have never met in person. We have been writing for several months, discussing possible business collaborations. One day, Dennis sent me an instant message and I began to type, "Hey Sweetie..." in reply. I suddenly realized that Dennis doesn't know me well enough to know that I call everyone in my world "sweetheart" and "honey" and other terms of endearment. I had to step out of my own world for a minute and imagine how being called "sweetie" could be construed when it is in writing, without the verbal intonation that indicates the innocence of the words. The same thing applies to signing e-mails "with love..." or "yours."

Jan once read me an e-mail that a man she was very interested in had sent after their initial meeting. The short e-mail said, "We'll have to get together again sometime." She asked me what I thought it meant, then proceeded to reread it several times, alternating the emphasis of the sentence: "We'll *have to* get together again sometime." "We'll have to *get together again* sometime." "We'll have to get together again *sometime.*" Surprised at how such a simple statement could mean so many different things? There is a high likelihood that the sender didn't think about the possible meanings anywhere near as much as Jan did. I'm sure he would be surprised, too!

    ▓ **If you are the one sending a message, let the person know what you really mean with a few carefully placed exclamation points, italics, or capital letters. In the world of e-mailing, capital letters are the equivalent of yelling and are only used for strong emphasis. Are your messages clear? Are your feelings adequately expressed via e-mail?**

In verbal communication, we rely heavily on intonation to convey meaning, but in e-mail we have only words, color, punctuation, and symbols to get our message across clearly. The number of words we use also carries a message. When someone takes time to post a paragraph versus a sentence, it gives the reader the impression that the message was important or heartfelt. While being verbose can overwhelm people in terms of volume and time commitment, not saying enough will certainly underwhelm them. Nick, a 46-year-old man, shared, "Online dating has taught me to break from self-centeredness and understand how people perceive me just through communication of words." This is a skill all of us can benefit from developing in order to minimize the effects of incorrect assumptions, whether online or off.

E-mail Emotions

A woman at my work sent me an e-mail that had me thinking she was mad at me. When I saw her, I asked her about her note, and she was surprised because she wasn't upset with me at all. She jokingly assured me that from that point on, should she ever be angry with me, she would write in capital letters and make them red so I would have no doubt as to her feelings.

Communicating mood and subtle nuances of emotion is almost impossible via e-mail without some specific writing skills. Authors paint pictures with their words for us all of the time, but not all of us have the time or talent for beautiful prose. Instead, there are some simple tools that can come in very handy.

Necessity has always been the mother of invention. Today, there is a growing visual vocabulary of punctuation marks that convey e-motions, or e-mail emotions. These icons, commonly referred to as "emoticons," are little faces that can be typed into e-mail and chats to let someone know how you are feeling or to convey the emotional context of your words.

Below you will find a list of a few of the more common emoticons. If you type "emoticons" into a keyword search on AOL, you'll get entire message boards from people who have invented hundreds of new emoticons. To see the face in these icons, tilt your head to the left. Depending on individual preferences, some people include a nose in their face, :-), while others do not, :).

Angel	0:-)
Angry	:-II
Angry and screaming	:-@
Angry, annoyed	>:-(
Bland face	:-1
Bored	:-o
Bummed out	:-c
Crying	:'-)
Evil	}-)
Friendly	:-]
Frowning	:-(
Frustrated	:-/
Glasses	8-)
Grinning	:-D
Hug	{ }
Kiss	:-*)
Kissing	:-x
Laughing	:-)))
Laughing tears	:.-)
Mouth wired shut	:-$
Mute	:-X
Not talking	:-I
Real downer	:-[

Shades	B-)
Shocked	=:-)
Sleeping	:-Z
Smiling	:-)
Surprised	:-O
Talking	:-()
Tongue out	:-P
Tongue-tied	:-&
Winking	;-)
Wry smile	:-}

Microsoft Word has become creative in helping with emoticons as well. If you hold down the shift key while typing a colon and parenthesis, ":)", it will type smiling or frowning symbols for you! Of course, simply using words to share your facial expressions also works. I am now so used to typing "smile" in e-mail correspondences that I have to resist doing the same thing in my other writing.

To speed up typing (and reading), online lingo now also includes abbreviations for terms that are often used in e-mail. "LOL," which stands for "laughing out loud," is one of the most widely used. Below is a list of some of the most common abbreviations. Whether or not you choose to use emoticons or abbreviations, I guarantee that if you spend much time online in chats or exchanging e-mails, someone will inevitably send them to you. In fact, you will undoubtedly encounter a variety of shortcuts using letters or numbers instead of words to form sentences, such as "C U 4 dinner." Making sense of the lingo online is similar to deciphering personalized license plates!

2U2	To You, Too
AFK	Away from Keyboard
ASAP	As Soon As Possible
BBL	Be Back Later
BOT	Back on Topic
BRB	Be Right Back
BTW	By the Way
C4N	Ciao for Now
CU	See You
CUL(8R)	See You Later
CWOT	Complete Waste of Time
CYA	See Ya
EOD	End of Discussion
EZ	Easy
F2F	Face-to-Face
FAQ	Frequently Asked Questions
FWIW	For What It's Worth
FYI	For Your Information
GAL	Get a Life
GBTW	Get Back To Work
GFC	Going for Coffee
GMTA	Great Minds Think Alike
GTG	Got to Go

GTRM	Going to Read Mail
GU	Geographically Undesirable
HAND	Have a Nice Day
IC	I See
IMHO	In My Humble Opinion
IMO	In My Opinion
IMPE	In My Previous/Personal Experience
IOW	In Other Words
IRL	In Real Life
ISP	Internet Service Provider
J/K	Just kidding
L8TR	Later
LOL	Laughing Out Loud
LTNS	Long Time No See
OTOH	On the Other Hand
OIC	Oh, I See
OLL	Online Love
PLS	Please
PU	That Stinks!
ROTFL	Rolling on the Floor Laughing
RUOK	Are You OK?
SO	Significant Other
THX	Thanks

TLK2UL8R	Talk to You Later
TWIMC	To Whom It May Concern
TXS	Thanks
URL	Web Page Address
WU?	What's up?
WWW	World Wide Web
ZZZ	Sleeping

▨ **How do you communicate your emotions and feelings in e-mail? Are you at ease using descriptive words, or would you feel better using shorthand, such as emoticons or abbreviations?**

A Personal Touch

Are there other ways to make an e-mail feel personal, more intimate? There sure are! As you read about the following conversation techniques, reflect on your own face-to-face and writing styles. Identify your personal repertoire for making people feel attended to as you add these skills to your personal communication toolbox.

One practice I recommend takes a lead from successful face-to-face encounters. You might say it is "name-calling" in the best possible sense. Addressing your pen pal by name and using their name periodically throughout your e-mail can make a correspondence feel more personal. Referring to someone by name in the middle of written conversation is the online equivalent of eye contact; it lets the other person know that you are speaking directly to them. By the same token, using their name in the e-mail or letter lets them know that you didn't cut and paste this same message to a hundred other people. Generally, people love to hear their names used in attentive and nurturing ways. Just be careful not to overdo it, or you risk sounding repetitive or aggressive.

One man, a 41-year-old cowboy, wrote to tell me how he adds a special personal touch to his online communications. "I have many women that would love to be with me, because I write songs for 'em and sing to 'em!" At the end of his e-mail, he even offered to write a song for me!

Another technique you will want in your conversational toolbox is the ability to speak specifically. Don't use meaningless or general words when you can say something specific. For example, receiving a note that says, "It was really fun," doesn't hold a candle romantically to "Meeting you was wonderful," or "Our day at the beach was relaxing and inspiring." Language is far more effective when we use the actual words we mean, whether verbally or in writing. If you replace "it" with what you are really trying to say, your communications will be clearer and carry more impact.

By the same token, we often use the word "you" when we really mean "I." For example, someone might say, "Sometimes you just feel like getting out of the house," when they really mean "Sometimes *I* just feel like...." Similarly, "You can stay online all night if you're not careful!" really means "I can stay online all night if I am not careful." By using "I" when we mean "I" we stand to become more self-aware and responsible for ourselves. By using "you" we distance ourselves from the meaning of our words, making the sentence generic rather than personal.

If we use our e-mail communications as a place to practice choosing powerful words that mean what we really want to say, we will be better able to do the same thing in our verbal language, as well. Consequently, our communication with others will become much more effective.

There is a professional technique used in the media called "blending," which I learned from my media coach, Joel Roberts. Blending requires that we listen for the words that another person uses in their questions or comments, and then use one or two of the same words in our response. When this happens, the words of both people get connected in such a way that they become a seamless flow of communication—a *blending* of conversation.

While Joel was talking specifically about radio and TV interviews, this technique has additional benefits for other communication. In e-mail or chats, blending helps the other person remember what they originally said to you or what you are responding to, as it is easy to forget from one e-mail to the next, especially if one is corresponding with several people. Blending also helps you listen more carefully and makes the other person feel heard.

A typical conversation might sound like this:

Suzanne: "What did you do last night?"

Joe: "Went to the movies."

Suzanne: "What'd you see?"

Joe: "*Creepy Crawlers*—scary."

Suzanne: "Ick. I like love stories."

We have the benefit of seeing the questions and responses on the same page, so this looks totally natural. However, in e-mail, the questions may have been sent 24 hours before the answers were delivered, and in a chat, several other comments may have been inserted in between answers, leaving room for confusion.

Alternately, blending might sound something like this—with the blended words in italics:

Suzanne: "What did you do last night?"

Joe: "*Last night,* I went to a movie."

Suzanne: "Oh, which *movie* did you see?"

Joe: "I saw *Creepy Crawlers*—a really scary *movie!*"

Suzanne: "I don't like *scary* movies; I like love stories."

This is a simplistic example, but you can see how blending weaves a thread of connection through the conversation, making it more complete than our typical communication. This may seem like a lot of work, but once you get the hang of incorporating key words into your responses, blending will become more natural and fun. Of course, attaching the previously sent e-mail message to your reply also helps tremendously in following a particular line of thought when hours or even days separate responses.

Communication is both sharing and listening, giving and receiving. Since the act of writing is more about sharing, commenting on the words of others shows that you have been listening. Let your recipients know that you have heard what they said and check by asking clarifying questions. By practicing these powerful skills on the Internet, you will be able to apply them more easily in face-to-face communication as well.

▨ **How do you add a personal touch to your writing? How can you apply that skill in your daily communications?**

Conscious Acts of Kindness

A few years ago, there was a movement in the U.S. to practice "random kindness and senseless acts of beauty" aided by a book on the same theme. The idea was to do nice things for no other purpose than to uplift someone else's day. It has been heartwarming to hear that people are doing that very thing via online dating.

Richard, a 33-year-old gentleman, wrote, "I like the ability to be more open than normal and to say things I couldn't in everyday life. I once complimented a lady who I could tell was a terrific, beautiful, and loving person, although I knew I had no chance of meeting her. I just thought it was the right thing to do." Other people have written to say how touched they were that someone would take the time to say things like, "I loved your profile; you seem great. Due to distance there is no chance, but good luck to you!"

If you are feeling down while you read profile after profile in search of a mate, make a point of letting the people whose messages mattered to you or who sounded wonderful but lived too far away, know that you noticed. Take the opportunity to transform other people's lives! Conscious kindness will switch your whole attitude while you are online. Sometimes a positive switch is all we need to turn our whole world around. See whose life you can brighten with your kind words and I'll bet you will find your own is brightened as well.

In his e-mail, Richard implied to me that he would not be inclined to compliment a stranger like that in person. But to hold back is a lost opportunity. After you have practiced saying kind things to people online, with no expectation of any return benefit to you, try it in person too. We are served by many people every day—in the market, the post office, a restaurant. Practice saying "thank you" to people who do a great job and make a difference in your day.

Being told that you look great by someone who isn't trying to get anything from you is the ultimate compliment. If doing this for someone you'd like to date is too big of a stretch, start with someone less scary. Tell the older lady in the market that her hair looks beautiful or that her outfit is a wonderful color. Practice acts of kindness where you feel safe and then spread out from there. Who knows what kind of conversation may get sparked, whom you may meet, or how your day may change as a result of giving to someone else.

Look for ways to perform acts of kindness throughout your day, online and off!

The Black Hole of Cyberspace

"I don't like not really connecting other than through the written word. It can be a very unsatisfying thing for someone like me, who likes to integrate the abstract and physical and emotional aspects of an individual in order to 'know' them."

ELLA, 47

"The only glaring inadequacy of Net dating is that communication does not take place eye-to-eye. Hence, it is difficult to ascertain the other party's truthfulness or mood. Because of that, communication skills need to be fine-tuned."

NICK, 48

"It is hard not getting immediate feedback on what I say in order to judge how it was taken. Things are left unsaid that I would normally say in person, to make sure they are not taken the wrong way."

GABRIEL, 33

"I think any time my partner is offering even the smallest amount of his time to another woman in any kind of romantic or sexual way—cyber or otherwise—that he is cheating. How can a man give 100 percent of himself to his partner if he shares those personal things with someone else too? The answer is he can't. Either he is devoted, or he is not."

CAITLIN, 22

10

"Getting Dumped" Has Never Been Simpler

"Sorry I didn't write back to you sooner.
Somehow your letter ended up in my trash."

JACK, 46

NE OF MY PET PEEVES in life is the use of the phrase "getting dumped" to mean "breaking up." I'd personally like to eliminate the use of these words in the context of relationships. We dump trash; we break up with people. However, this phrase, ironically, has never been more appropriate than with the advent of online dating. That little recycle bin or trash can icon on the desktop has received many a rejected paramour's e-mail—never in our lives has it been easier to put a relationship in the can.

As with any relationship, online relationships have both benefits and challenging moments of doubt, miscommunication, deception, and loneliness. All of the tools we have discussed in this book so far—a personal code of ethics, skills for self-observation, enhanced self-esteem and communication, aligning your choices with your goals—will come in handy when you encounter what I refer to as "the black hole" of cyberspace. These tools will help you both to handle rejection and to let others down graciously. In this chapter, let's explore how to handle the emotional emergencies that can accompany communication breakdowns: making assumptions, projection, and rejection.

The Numbers Game

There is nothing quite so disheartening as scanning a million profiles, setting your sights on the man or woman who interests you most, agonizing over the exact wording of your message to them, sending it off with hope, and then...no response, or "thanks, but no thanks."

In a workshop I once attended, we did an interesting exercise on rejection. We were instructed to walk around the room asking everyone for something we wanted. Everyone was to say "no" to the first nine people who approached them, and "yes" to the tenth person. I roamed around asking and being rejected over and over again, while at the same time rejecting those who were asking me, and I could hear "yes" being said to other people all around me. As all the participants became aware of the "yes" responses that were circulating, an energy started building in the room: it was only a matter of time before we would get one—or give one. What started out as depressing transformed into something hopeful and exciting with only a subtle shift in attitude.

Dating on the Internet is a bit like this exercise. One woman, Kelly, explained to me that she operates on a statistic that says the odds are you have relationship potential with one person out of every fifty. "The way I figured, it would take far too much time to meet fifty people during the course of my regular life, but by going online I could 'meet' fifty people in no time. Strictly by the odds, my chances seem better online."

Mitch, a man in his 50s, writes, "Online dating seemed like a very reasonable way to play the numbers game. I targeted one to three women every few weeks (assuming the previous set did not work out). This was how many I could focus on given the limited but reasonable amount of time I wanted to put into it. I did this until I met my girlfriend. You have to know what you want, though, read other people's descriptions carefully, and keep up a meaningful dialog to find out more."

One man, 38, said he tried online dating by sending out four-teen e-mails to people whose profiles interested him. "Of those fourteen, twelve were unanswered and two were 'no thanks.'" Then he quit. If we quit looking after passing fourteen potential dates on the street who were not interested in return, we would never meet anyone. Dating, whether online or off, requires that we are perse-vering, proactive, and persistent.

> What kind of strategy are you willing to use to approach online dating? Are you going to do it haphazardly, or are you going to follow a specific plan for finding love online?

Is It a "Projection of Rejection" or the "Real Deal"?

Rejection is an ugly beast. In the early phases of dating online every-thing seems personal, and so every rejection, or perceived rejection, can sting. After a while we begin to understand the nature of the beast and don't take rejection so personally. The challenge is for those who have been dating online for a long time not to give up hope.

The ironic part of online dating is this: you should take every-thing personally that *you* do, feel, think, post, and send, and take nothing personally that *anyone else* says or does to you. What, after all, really happens to your e-mail once you've pressed "send"? Who have you really sent the message to? Sure, you can easily *imagine* that Prince Charming or Ms. Perfect has read your e-mail and hasn't responded because you aren't good enough, but in actuality that may not be what happens at all!

There are thousands of men and women who put themselves into a major funk over an e-mail that evokes no response. Says Mar-sha, "People sometimes get mad if I don't answer their e-mail within 24 hours! What these guys don't understand is that I often get between fifty and a hundred e-mails a day!" Another woman, Dawn, received over four hundred responses to her profile. Of the men who responded, she opted to meet just twelve. "I wasn't able to spend the time needed to respond to all the e-mails *and* make arrangements to meet," she said. Charlene also received so many e-mail responses to her profile on a daily basis that she couldn't even open them anymore. "I used to respond to let them know that I wasn't interested, but I couldn't keep up. I feel bad, but I just delete them."

Not only can you not be certain whether your e-mail has been read, you also can't know *who* has read your message. One man wrote to me explaining, "The disadvantage of online dating is that because it is anonymous, you never know who you are really writing to on the other end. For example, I run fan club sites for several supermodels. *I* am the one who answers their e-mail and fulfills the chat requests. Most of the men really think they are talking with one of these beauties."

"Projection" is what happens when we attribute our own attitudes, or feelings, to someone else. When we blame the "event" for our response to it, we are projecting. In the case of an unanswered e-mail, we may think that someone is rejecting us and feel hurt, when in fact they may have done nothing at all. We have assumed the rejection and thus created our own hurt.

I experience this same challenge building online business relationships. I once spent 2 or 3 months working with a man named Mark from an online dating company, negotiating the use of *Intellectual Foreplay* on its site. We were getting close to closing an agreement, when suddenly he didn't write back anymore. My first reaction was to think I was being "dumped." A host of typical self-doubting thoughts emerged, along with assumptions that the company didn't like my book and was going to choose someone else to work with. After a short pity party, I decided to call again rather than give up. As it turned out, Mark had left the company. None of my self-defeating assumptions were true, and I was able pick up the pieces with his replacement. The whole experience of rejection took place solely in my head.

How often do we project our challenges in our face-to-face relationships? Projecting our fears onto other people and making assumptions that may or may not be accurate are choices that contribute hugely to our sense of despair and hopelessness. As the saying goes, "To assume (ass-u-me) is to make an ass out of you and me!"

> ▨ **Pay attention when you feel pain as a result of relationships. Are your feelings based on something real or imaginary? Do you know or are you assuming?**

Dive Within

When I first learned to scuba dive, one of the things that impressed me the most was that no matter how turbulent the surface conditions of the sea were, just a few feet below, the water became very calm and still. From that particular vantage point, I could look up and see the boat being tossed around on the waves or see rain drops splashing on the surface, but I was no longer *in* the chaos. I was in a place of tranquility, taking deep, calming breaths, which opened me up to a different perspective and more insight. This is the same process I suggest you follow whenever you encounter a drama in your life: dive within to find the place of tranquility inside you that is removed from the chaos.

> ▨ **Take several breaths, self-observe, and look for a different perspective.**

By doing this for even a split second when you receive an unpleasant or rejecting e-mail or when a date goes badly or when self-doubt or negative self-talk bubble up, you will be able to reconnect with who you really are, your values, your soul. That is the place of strength from which you can continue your search for a mate. There is no need to make life a live version of the "Jerry Springer Show"!

Dishing It Out

In the last chapter I spoke to you about choosing your words carefully to be sure they deliver the message that you really mean to send. Here I will suggest that you consider your words carefully because they can also act like arrows shot right into someone's heart—and I don't mean the Cupid variety! The idea that someone whom you have never met could feel so strongly about you that your words would hurt them deeply may be hard to imagine. Always remember that hope, more than anything, is what is at stake in the online dating world. When you say cruel things, you are crushing hope. When you say thoughtless or unconscious things, you may be contributing to someone's pain.

Here, for your consideration, is an excerpt from *Intellectual Foreplay*, which offers some thoughts about the power of our words.

> When we string together the correct letters to form a word that carries a certain impact in the world, we call it "spelling." When someone wants to create a magical impact in the world, they string certain letters or symbols together to create a "spell." Our words are very powerful. They are felt for many years after the moment of utterance. When words are strung together, we call the result a "sentence." Our words can literally "sentence" someone to a life of feeling pain or pleasure. When you communicate with your partner, be careful that what you say is the "spell" that you mean to cast.

When communicating with strangers over the Internet, it is easy to disassociate ourselves from the impact of our words. We don't see the other person's pain, and so we don't have to feel the guilt. As one woman pointed out, "You have to remember that *there is a person experiencing those words* who will be hurt if you say something cruel." In an online professional association of which I am a member, I am repeatedly surprised at how rudely people write—publicly—about other members. Just because we can't see another person doesn't mean we can't hurt them. If your intent is to hurt someone, consider whether that is the most effective way to bring about the result you desire, a way that is in alignment with your heart, not your ego.

In the E + R = OS model, a person could blow off their personal responsibility for how they treat others by saying, "Hey, I'm just the event. Others need to respond better." But there is more to it than that. While we are all responsible for how we respond to things people say to us, we are also custodians of each other's hearts. This responsibility should never be taken lightly.

When I was a teenager, my brother and I threw a big Halloween party. We had had big parties in the past and they had all gone well, but this one turned out differently. We didn't know who the guests were because everyone was in costume. The anonymity allowed people to steal things and act obnoxiously, people who would never have conducted themselves that way had they been identifiable.

The Internet can be like one big costume party in which everyone feels freer to do and say things that they would not do and say otherwise. Rather than using that anonymity to let out our darker side, why not use it to do *kind* things that we might not do otherwise! As responsible people, we need to do our part: we must act in alignment with our personal ethics *all of the time,* regardless of whether anyone is watching or not.

> ▦ **Be conscious of what you say. Deliver your message in alignment with your personal code of ethics. If you act unconsciously online and do not take responsibility for your impact on others, this habit will spill over into your face-to-face interactions, making it difficult if not impossible to create healthy, loving relationships in your life.**

Fifty Ways to Delete Your Lover

When you are faced with ending a correspondence or a relationship, or telling someone that you aren't interested in meeting them, *do so in the way that you imagine they would want to hear the message.* The Golden Rule, "Do unto others as you would have them do unto you," certainly applies here, but it is not sufficient. In some cases what you would have others "do unto you" may still be an unacceptable way to treat them. Many people have low self-esteem and, as a result, allow others to treat them in a thoughtless or unkind manner. Others with high self-esteem may not care what someone says to them. People's definitions of inappropriate behavior vary, and rude comments are often camouflaged in hurtful "humor." Consequently, the Golden Rule needs the addition of: "and do unto others as *they would have you* do unto them." In order to know this, though, you need to communicate.

Hundreds of people I have interviewed say they want to be let down "politely, honestly, and respectfully." They prefer to be told "straight" and don't want to be "left hanging" or wondering about an e-date's intentions. While just not responding to a suitor is a common practice because it's "easy," "guiltless," or "time efficient," it can feel very rude on the receiving end.

Opinions about this vary greatly, however. A woman in her 30s says, "Why mail someone to try to tell them nicely that you're not interested? Nothing you say will feel nice to them. You're better off just leaving them alone to find someone else." Says another woman, "Just tell me! It isn't a personal thing. It's like interviewing someone for a job. Sometimes it's a fit and sometimes it isn't. Knowing is better than wondering if they're just too busy to e-mail. If they don't tell me, I don't know when to give up!" Adds a third, "Either way is fine with me, since it's not like a 'real' rejection."

One thing to keep in mind when you are on the receiving end is that, while a rejection may not actually be a rejection of *you,* no news is probably not good news. If someone doesn't respond to an e-mail, there may be a hundred reasons, none of which you really need to know, but all of which mean "not interested in a relationship." Don't flog a dead horse! If you are really inspired, you can send a follow-up e-mail to be sure that your original message was received—maybe take a slightly different approach—but if there is still no response, move on.

■ **The Numbers Game means that every "no" brings you that much closer to a "yes!"**

The following list of "Fifty Ways to Delete Your Lover" has been compiled from actual online experiences and many are direct quotes or suggestions. One woman told me, "I just tell people I'm not interested, but there are variations in degree, from 'let's be friends' to 'you are a freak' or 'you need mental help.' It really depends on the situation!" Another woman exclaimed, "One time when I was honest, the guy came back at me ranting and said some pretty nasty things. That's when I decided it is probably better just not to write back." Elizabeth offers this advice, "Remember, Mr. Delete Key is often a girl's best friend, along with his relatives, Mr. Block Sender and Mr. Filter!" Of course, there is no right or wrong way to get out of an online liaison, just ways that are in alignment with you, your ethics, and your goals. Use the list below to get your creative juices flowing.

1. Don't respond.

2. Become scarce until they lose interest.

3. Sound uninterested and then ignore them.

4. Say you are disinterested clearly, diplomatically, and as soon as possible.

5. Point out something specific in their profile that doesn't work for you: "I don't date people who have kids," or are divorced, or are long-distance, etc.

6. Tell the truth.

7. "Let's just be friends."

8. "Thank you for your note. I am not available at present. Hope you find your real mate soon."

9. "I'm already writing to too many people, but thank you."

10. "I'm not interested, thank you."

11. "You're not my type."

12. "Sorry, I realized that I am not over my last partner yet. I am not ready for a new relationship."

13. "I don't think a relationship with you would meet my most important needs."

14. "I'm not really interested in pursuing this, but it was nice to meet you."

15. "It was very nice to meet you, but I don't feel any chemistry between us. I hope you find someone that you connect with."

16. "It was nice to meet you, but it's not a good fit for me. Best of luck in your search."

17. "Sorry, I'm going to be really busy for awhile."

18. "I believe you are a very nice person, but I don't think we would connect face-to-face. I wish you luck!"

19. Compliment them, then explain, "I have gotten back into a relationship with someone I met before you—sorry."

20. "Thank you for your interest, I am flattered by the compliment. However, I am interested in someone else at this time. I wish you all the luck in finding someone compatible."

21. "Thank you for writing. I'm seeing several people right now and do not have time for more."

22. "Critical Differences. Thank you."

23. "I already found someone."

24. "I'm gay."

25. "You're not what I am looking for."

26. "I'm going to be out of town for a while."

27. "Thank you, but I've stopped looking for love on the Internet."

28. "I'm married."

29. "You live in Australia and I live in Alaska, so it won't work."

30. "I'm not interested in getting serious right now. Let's cool it before things progress."

31. "I'm looking for someone younger."

32. "I'm looking for someone older."

33. "Thank you, but no thank you. Good luck."

34. In order not to hurt their feelings, mention things about yourself that they won't like: "I don't believe in God or marriage, and I think drug legalization is the way to go."

35. Send them the "vibe."

36. Block them out of your instant messenger program.

37. Change your online name.

38. Disappear.

39. Decline to meet them.

40. Tell them you "suddenly have to go," and click off of instant messenger.

41. Tell them your computer keeps crashing.

42. "I'm very flattered but I'm looking for something a little different."

43. "Sorry, this doesn't feel like a match. Good luck on your journey!"

44. Put a stopper to romantic or sexy talk.

45. "I'm sorry, you seem like a really nice person, but I'm not interested."

46. "Sorry, it is not working out. I don't want to hurt you and lead you on. Good luck and hope you find someone."

47. "No, thank you. Please don't ask again."

48. "No. If you persist, I will complain to Sys Admin."

49. "I'm sorry, I only date people with an IQ in the positive integers."

50. "I'm short, fat, ugly, and I stink!"

> As you determine how you would "delete your lover," imagine how it would feel if these things were being done or said to you. Choose methods in alignment with your ethics and add them to your repertoire. Would you make a different choice if you were looking in the person's eyes?

A few online dating sites have "Breakup Generators," which you can click on to get help composing a breakup e-mail. While they are entertaining gadgets to play with, the breakup notes they tend to generate are not very respectful and wouldn't be much fun to receive, just as some of the messages above would not. I concur with a woman in her 30s who said, "Don't ever leave a person feeling downhearted. It is your job to lift them up—unless you want it to come back on you. Respect breeds respect."

"I" Statements

When you need to let someone down, whether online or in person, take responsibility for your feelings; don't blame them on the other person. Your lack of interest is because of you, not them. The process of finding a match is *not* about finding what is right and wrong in the other person, but rather, what is right and wrong *for you.*

You can convey this difference to your e-dates easily by using "I" statements, or sentences that begin with "I" instead of "you." Rather than saying "You are too old" or "You are not my type," use "I" statements that claim what is *true for you,* not what you *perceive to be wrong with them.* For example, "I'm looking for someone younger" and "I'm not interested in a cyber sex relationship." There are a couple of benefits to this approach. Owning your feelings is more truthful and less hurtful. After all, you are sharing your *opinions or preferences,* not facts. Beauty is in the eye of the beholder. There may be someone else who is looking for the very attributes that you are turning away from.

Another benefit of using "I" statements is that your suitor will have a harder time arguing with you about your reasons for turning them down. If you say, "I'm looking for someone younger," they will realize it's not an issue of trying to persuade you that they are younger than they seem or in good shape for their age. Your comment is not about them, but rather about your goals and desires. If they do try to sell you on their wonderful youthful qualities, you can politely explain, "I understand, but my decision is not about you. Your age is perfect, just not for me. Thank you."

The point is to avoid the blame game that is inherent in the use of "you statements." Again, this skill—which must be practiced—is *very* applicable in our face-to-face relationships, as well. Eliminating "you statements" from your communication will greatly contribute to maintaining healthy relationships. By respectfully owning your opinions, desires, likes, and dislikes, you will open the door for better and clearer communication in all your relationships.

▓ Take responsibility for what you want and what you don't want. Use "I" statements that align your words with your feelings.

▓ What do "I" statements sound like in your family relationships? In your business relationships? In your intimate and romantic relationships?

11

Untangling the Web

P RIOR TO THE INTERNET, the word "web" was primarily associated with spiders. Their intricate threadlike creations are fascinating to behold and are often quite elaborate. Webs provide spiders with the ability to travel and maneuver—in this they are much like our highways. At the same time, webs serve as sticky traps to catch prey for a spider's supper.

While the Internet was dubbed the World Wide Web for its amazing ability to connect us to one another, the Web can also be woven into elaborate traps. As online dating has gained in popularity it has inevitably attracted people with ulterior motives. People both young and old, savvy and naïve, have walked into traps set by others with false identities. The Web has also opened a door to unique temptations: relationship infidelities of all kinds and serious computer addictions that range from obsessively going online or checking e-mail to spending huge amounts of time in sexually related sites and chats.

In this chapter we'll look at the flip side of the Web—how the positive aspects of the Internet can turn negative, and how you can avoid the seduction of unhealthy behaviors.

An Ounce of Prevention Is the Best Cure

If how you use the Internet ever begins to interfere with your real life, stop and take a serious look at what you are doing. The Internet is a tool; not a goal or a value in and of itself. If we're not careful, our desire for online companionship can actually take us away from physical companionship. We can easily get absorbed in our computers, leaving no time for real-life connections. Even Steve and I find ourselves sitting back-to-back facing our individual computers for long periods of time, rather than engaging with each other.

One woman pointed out to me that if her ex-husband had put as much time and energy into their marriage as he gave to his online chats, their marriage could have survived. Another man stated the obvious: that the very act of sitting at a computer all day is not good for the body, the means with which we connect with others in relationships. If we use the magnificent tool that the Web is unconsciously, without balance, we can easily destroy relationships rather than enhance them. If intimate, loving relationships are what you want, it may be that you need to *stop seeking* and *start seeing* the opportunities all around you.

There are two considerations involved: one is *how much* time is being spent online, the other is *how* your time is being spent online. Here are some steps that you can take to avoid getting caught in the Web. Once again, the Internet is a perfect practice ground for skills that can be applied offline as well.

1. Become aware of how much time you are spending on the Internet, what you are doing online, and the effect this is having on your life and relationships.

2. Clearly set your intentions, goals, and time lines for using the Web. Give yourself a reasonable allotment of time in which to participate online and honor your self-set limits. Use a timer if need be. Be self-observant, making sure that your actions are in alignment with your goals.

3. Commit yourself to choosing practices that are in alignment with your personal code of ethics and that support your well-being, as well as the well-being of others in your life.

4. Practice self-control and moderation. As with television, drugs, alcohol, gambling, shopping, eating, and sex, we need to practice and develop self-control in order to avoid becoming addicted. The Internet puts several of these things right at our fingertips, all in the same package, requiring an even higher level of self-responsibility than with any one addictive activity. For some of us, not ever getting started is the best prevention. For others, conscious moderation is all that is needed.

5. Evaluate your life for balance of body, mind, and spirit. If you find your life is skewed, pay attention to the aspects that need more time. The goal is mental, emotional, spiritual, and physical health. You will be more attractive to others if your life is in balance.

Intimacy Starvation

When we hear the word "intimacy," most people immediately think of the physical intimacy of a sexual encounter. There is another form of intimacy, however, that human beings crave, one that is elusive for many. This is the intimacy of the spirit—an interweaving of two people through sharing their hearts and souls. Many have tried finding it through sex, mistaking one form of intimacy for another, but that hasn't worked. Others have sought it in multiple partners and that hasn't worked either. Many are now searching for intimacy online. We continue to search outside of ourselves for the source of intimacy, for the perfect set of circumstances—a new partner, a new position, a bigger high, a greater thrill. When we find what we think we are searching for, the excitement is often short-lived, and we are left feeling distraught and empty again. The same old story haunts us all—the highs diminish in intensity, the marriage gets boring, and the sex loses its passion.

While the Internet can be a great place to find people with whom we may be able to *share* intimacy, intimacy itself cannot be found there. So what are we doing wrong? We are going on a treasure hunt for something we think we can *find*, when in actuality, *intimacy is a creative process*. Instead of seeking this depth of connection outside ourselves, we need to draw from "the well within" and bring forth intimacy into our relationships—our real-life relationships and friendships. Intimacy, you could say, is an "inside job."

The Latin roots of the word "intimate" are *intimare*, meaning "to make known," and *intimus*, meaning "innermost." In a play on the word, intimacy can be heard as "in to me see." When we seek intimacy we want someone to look into our very souls, to recognize who we are and to love us, unconditionally, regardless of what we do or how we look. When we connect on an intimate level our experience goes beyond the physical, the surface touch of our skins, to the metaphysical, a sharing of our true selves, a dance of our souls. By accessing this aspect of our own beings, we become able to share ourselves with our partner in a truly intimate way.

Studies have shown that human beings also need physical touch to thrive and that intimacy, both physical and spiritual, is critical to our health. Dr. Dean Ornish, heart specialist and author of *Love and Survival: The Scientific Basis for the Healing Power of Intimacy,* said in a television interview, "I don't know anything in medicine, including diet, drugs, or surgery, that has a greater impact on our health and premature death and disease as the healing power of love and intimacy." He went on to say, "Study after study has shown that people who feel lonely, depressed, and isolated have three to five times the rate of premature death and disease, across the board, when compared to those who have a sense of love and connection and community. And study after study is showing that when we open our hearts to each other, when we find ways of becoming more intimate, not just in romantic relationships but in any kind of relationship, it is healing." Others studies have concurred, citing greater happiness and longer life spans among those who live with others, thereby receiving nurturing touch and support on a regular basis. When the two forms of intimacy are experienced together, the results are phenomenal—long, happy lives full of unconditional love, health, and self-satisfaction.

Counter to our needs, our society and culture are constantly selling us on the benefits of being shallow rather than going deeper. Just like the ease and convenience of disposable goods and fast food, we have the ability to engage in virtual relationships and virtual sex without actually connecting with another human being face-to-face, heart-to-heart, body-to-body. If our "partner" says something wrong, we can "delete" them as we might eliminate an imaginary creature in a video game, with the press of a button. But this is not the way it works in our real lives. If we are unable to transition virtual companionship to our personal world, we will remain empty and unfulfilled.

If your only intimate relationships are with strangers online, take a serious look at what you are creating. This is the time to look in the mirror, do some self-observation, work on your self-esteem, stretch your personality, take some risks, get off the computer, and get into your life.

A Meeting of the Minds

As I conducted interviews for this book, I was continuously amazed by—and grateful for—the number of people, many of whom I have never met, who shared deeply personal experiences and stories with me. Ironically, the things we wouldn't tell someone face-to-face are our truth: our vulnerabilities, our dreams, our desires, and our stories. We pour our hearts out to total strangers and feel like we know them more deeply than anyone else in our lives. Is this because we met them on the Internet? No. It's because we have dared to share our innermost selves, the things we think in our own quiet moments.

This level of intimate disclosure is freeing, releasing us from being the only bearer of the burden of our thoughts. This kind of communication, this meeting of the minds and sharing of the hearts, is what we are hungering for in our face-to-face relationships.

The online dating industry seems to be filling an unexpected demand for a kind of therapy, as a means of catharsis or emotional cleansing, with strangers. The process of self-disclosure is similar to that of making a confession in church. Sherry, a college student conducting research on Internet dating, tells me that many of the people she interviews put her in the role of therapist, telling her their problems and asking for advice. This sort of layman's therapy could be a wonderful thing or a disaster, depending on to whom you open your heart, how they deal with what you tell them, how you deal with their response, and whether you are able to learn something valuable to apply in your life. The bottom line is that we are reaching out to other people, sharing ourselves, and hoping for love and acceptance. The Internet is a great place to *practice* this level of communication.

We need to begin opening up more in our face-to-face relationships, as well. We spend a lot of time and energy creating and maintaining masks that keep people from knowing our true feelings in an effort to avoid being hurt. This filter to keep hurt out keeps love out very effectively, too. If you find that you are enjoying deep or revealing discussions on the Net, start having deeper and more meaningful conversations with the people in your daily life. Take the risk and see what happens. Of course, not every person or every moment of your day is appropriate for this depth of connection. Use your head as to when and where, but begin integrating this kind of honest communication into your relationships.

If you want people to open their hearts to you in real life, though, you will have to remember to honor confidentiality with a passion. One reason anonymity on the Internet is so attractive is that no one can break confidentiality. There is no need for trust, because no one knows who you are. If someone throws something back in your face later, you can always stop communicating with them—you don't have to have the skills to resolve the problem. In face-to-face relationships, if someone puts you down for something you share or uses sarcasm in communicating with you, you will not feel safe sharing yourself with them anymore. The same is true for your responses to people who share with you—you cannot expect someone to open up to you if you are sitting in judgement of them. The level of intimacy you seek in person has to be earned with trust. You will need to take the risk to trust others, as well.

> ▨ **Take your online ability to share your heart into your everyday life. Increase the quality of your communication. Practice online, apply offline.**

> ▨ **Explore what it is that you enjoy about using the Internet. Is it the depth of communication? The ease and convenience? The anonymity? The variety? The entertainment? By simply being aware of what you are drawn to you will be able to take steps to incorporate those features into your face-to-face relationships. Or, at the very least, by knowing what things are calling to you, you will be able to make conscious decisions about their importance in your life.**

Easy Infidelity

As one friend said when I told him I was exploring online dating sites as research for this book, "Be careful not to get sucked into the belly of the beast!" I assured him I was in no danger, but his warning is a good one. Having thousands of available men and women at your fingertips on the computer can provide you with an easy opportunity to be disloyal—literally with the click of a button!

As I navigated many online dating services, reading profiles and gathering information, it became obvious that there are quite a few married people online, looking for something outside their marriage. While some may be lying about their marital status, others are quite up-front about their intentions. One man took the time to explain to me why he was looking for something "meaningful and discreet" online: "My marriage is really over, but because of the kids and our financial situation, getting officially divorced right now just won't work. It's going to take me a couple of years to extricate myself from the situation. I'm looking for someone who is willing to be the 'other woman' in the meantime, who understands and is willing to put up with my circumstances for the time being."

A woman in her 40s wrote and said, "My husband was addicted to cyber sex via e-mail. I was not aware of that until I ran across some of his e-mail printouts. I felt hurt and betrayed. What he wrote was graphic and very intimate. I think what hurt the most is that he told all these women he loved them. That was the ultimate betrayal." Sid shared remorse over his own behavior: "I am now divorced because I was cheating on my ex-wife over the Net. I know if she ever took me back, I would not repeat that mistake." This kind of infidelity is certainly not limited to men. Angela, a woman in her 30s, tells me, "I was having cyber sex while I was married. My ex-husband hated me talking like that online and it ultimately played a role in our divorce." Another man said, "I broke up with a partner of 7 years because she didn't feel that cyber sex outside of our relationship was wrong, but then she followed through and met some of the people, which led to sex offline."

Infidelity is not reserved solely for married people. A young man wrote that he lost his girlfriend, whom he had met online and was seeing exclusively, when she logged on to the dating site on which they had met and found his profile still listed with a new photo posted. She felt that he must have been fishing for new love interests—why else would he have posted a new picture? However, when he asked her why she had logged on to the site herself, she excused it as "woman's intuition."

▨ **If you commit to an exclusive relationship, either list that change clearly in your profile or take your profile off the site until you are available again.**

For some people, this is an unexpected arena in which addiction to the Internet arises. Voluntarily putting a stop to all the attention that one can receive via e-mail can be hard to do. Meeting new people is fun. Making friends is wonderful. Receiving compliments and romantic interest feels good. However, it becomes deceptive and destructive—both to your partner and your e-mail pals—when you are unavailable and yet stay listed on a dating site.

What constitutes cheating can get a bit vague when you are in a relationship with someone you have never met. One man, who was in a long-distance relationship with a woman he'd never met who lived in another country, felt tremendous guilt when he "cheated on her" with a woman who lived in his area. He ended up breaking up with the woman nearby in order to be true to his cyber girlfriend, even though he anticipated that he would never get to meet her in person because she lived so far away and their cultures were so different. A man from another country wrote to tell me that his wife took him to court and had his cyber mistress legally deemed his actual mistress in their divorce case, even though he had never met her face-to-face!

When your cyber connections are interfering with your real-life relationships, you need to carefully consider what your goals are and what approach is most likely to help you meet those goals. As one man pointed out, "The computer is fine for e-mail, but for in-the-body love, get your body near the bodies you want in your life."

Another man had a particularly creative solution to the issue of cheating. He explained that if his partner were particularly interested in having cyber sex, he would happily volunteer to go into the other room and type to her from there!

When the Grass Is Greener

You're probably all familiar with the adage "The grass is always greener on the other side." Single people wish to be in a committed relationship, married people wish to be single, or worse yet, they both want someone else's spouse. Online, this plays out as: the guy online sounds better than the boyfriend at home, and your girlfriend in Russia seems better than your wife. Again, this is a matter of perspective. It is looking outside for the solutions, rather than looking within for the answers.

> **If the grass is greener on the other side, water your own lawn! Offer nourishment and it will grow.**

If you are reading this book, chances are you aren't currently in a committed relationship. When you are, though, post the above words on your refrigerator as a constant reminder. When things get rough in a relationship, our society encourages us to just give up and move on. With so many options so immediately accessible on the Internet, this has never been easier to do. In some cases, moving on is exactly what we should do. In other cases, though, so much could be done if we would take responsibility for what we are creating, honor our commitments, and bring out the elation in our *relation*ships.

> **Have an online love affair—with your partner or spouse! If you're already in a relationship, use e-mail, chats, and instant messages to add a new spark of romance to your relationship.**

Barry, a man in his 40s, told me that since he works out of his home and his wife works in a downtown office, they've begun using e-mail to communicate during the day. "I discovered aspects of my wife's personality—especially her sense of humor—that I hadn't really noticed before. Writing to each other is helping us to discover new things about each other!" These new discoveries are enhancing their relationship and keeping it fresh. Likewise, since I travel quite a bit, Steve and I also use e-mail and instant messages to stay in touch while I'm gone. Even after 10 years of being together, my heart still skips a beat when I see that he is online at the same time I am.

A reporter who was interviewing me for a newspaper article once said, "All this E + R = OS stuff sounds great if your partner is willing to participate." I can see how people might think a partner would have to be willing to put in at least 50 percent of the effort to turn a relationship around, but it isn't true. While it is preferable that both people give their all to mending a relationship, amazing things can happen if just one person takes responsibility for their part. Relationships are a system. One part is connected and responds to the other part. When one person shifts their behavior, the other person necessarily shifts as well.

In one of her shows, Oprah Winfrey featured a book called *How to Behave So Your Children Will, Too!,* by Dr. Sal Severe. This is a great title because it beautifully points out that how parents behave affects (and perhaps even dictates) how their children behave. When parents shift what they do, children shift in relationship to them. The same holds true in romantic relationships.

▓ Behave the way you want your partner to behave!

If you are experiencing a lack of intimacy in your life, an addiction to the Internet, or infidelity in your relationships, go back and reread Chapters 4 and 5 on taking personal responsibility for your choices and enhancing your self-esteem. Take the time to actually *do* the exercises in this book, rather than just reading them. Just as you are taking a proactive approach to finding a life partner, take a proactive approach to living in balance.

If you are in a relationship with someone who is displaying any of these behaviors, remember that is the "event." Your response options are to negotiate for change, resist your partner's behavior, accept your partner's behavior, or get out of the relationship. Look at *your choices,* rather than the other person's behavior, as the challenge before you. By doing so you will be empowered to create a solution *for you.* If you are finding that these behaviors—yours or someone else's—are impairing your life and you can't alter them yourself, seek professional help. Life is simply too short to waste.

Moving from Virtual to Physical

"The aspect I like most about online dating is that looks and physical attraction don't take part in the initial introduction of becoming acquainted with someone new. I learned about many aspects of the person's personality and characteristic traits without the obstacle of appearances."

JENNIFER, 31

"I learned the hard way that to date this way, do not spend too much time before meeting or at least getting a recent photo. I talked to someone for months, got really interested, and when we met, he was 400 pounds and had a bad attitude in person."

CHANTAL, 42

"Online dating is a brilliant way of getting to know someone, but there is no substitute for the real thing. You can only discover a character when you are face-to-face with the person for longer periods."

GREG, 43

12

Close Encounters

YNTHIA, 25, WAS SHOCKED to find flowers on her doorstep from her online suitor. Even though it was a nice gesture, she hadn't told him where she lived, and his having figured it out made her really nervous. "I hadn't realized that I had said what I did for a living in my profile 6 months earlier, and in one e-mail I had mentioned the company I worked for and in another the town that I lived in. He put two and two together and found out my name and address. I'm just lucky that he was a nice guy. He taught me to be a lot more careful about what I tell someone."

We have all heard the tragic stories that can happen when bad people get a hold of too much information online, or when adequate care and caution aren't used in a first-time meeting. A lot of effort has been put into educating Internet users about the necessity of being careful. As you venture from online to offline dating, take advantage of the safety nets that have been put into place to protect you. If you are a man thinking that this doesn't apply to you, think again. You do not know the actual identity or even the sex of the person you will be meeting. In addition, you don't know if there is a group of people behind that sweet voice online. There is no doubt about it—it pays to be cautious.

Many websites can provide you with extensive safety tips, including ways to conduct background checks on suitors or register who you are going out with and where you are meeting. It is my hope that the suggestions in this chapter and the tools that you will take away from this book will help you develop your own safe-dating protocol.

Playing It Safe

With online dating, asking for a reference before you meet is reasonable, but keep in mind it's not foolproof. One woman told me a story about a man who claimed he was divorced and even had his "ex-wife" call to tell her that he was indeed divorced and that he was a good man. She proceeded to get seriously involved with him and came home one day to find her house robbed and her bank account cleaned out. Apparently, his "ex" wasn't really an ex-wife but a partner he was in cahoots with to scam unsuspecting women.

In reality, the dangers of online dating are no greater than dating in person—perhaps even less so. Although dating always makes people vulnerable, the Internet has simply made us more aware of dating safety issues in general. Traditionally, a man would pick up a woman from her home for a first date, and we wouldn't have thought twice about handing a cute stranger our phone number for a potential date. Now, with the publicity about date rapes and scam artists, we are much more cautious. In person we have the advantage of being able to assess the person's appearance, but we must always be careful. Looks can be deceiving.

One true difference about online dating is that you don't really know the age or sex of the person who you are dialoging with, and virtually *anyone* can read your profile, discovering personal information. The Internet is available to everyone. No one is checking IDs at the door. While you control how much information you give out, to whom and how soon, it is easy to believe someone you've been dialoging with regularly is a trustworthy friend.

There have been stories in the news of adults who were lied to by minors and who then got into trouble with the law when they engaged in cyber sex or met their "date" in person. The opposite also happens. One woman wrote to me hopeful that if she shared her daughter's story other kids would be protected from the same horrible experience. "My 15-year-old daughter was online with a man who said he was 19. He repeatedly told her that he loved her and wanted to meet. He finally convinced her that she should meet him, so she lied and sneaked out of the house. When she showed up at the meeting place, he smooth-talked her into his car. He then had control and he raped her."

While this young girl's story is terrible, and I wish that such behavior had never taken place, the fact that she met her rapist on the Internet probably isn't that relevant. Having counseled teens for years, I know they get into dangerous situations with strangers far more often than their parents would like to believe. Care and safety issues for dating extend far beyond the Net. The added challenge, in this case, was that this man was able to pull on a young girl's heart-strings with promises of love *prior* to meeting, which made her more vulnerable and trusting. These dangers are not restricted to the young; I have heard stories of the same level of risk-taking and vulnerability from adult women in their 30s and 40s.

We need to be careful on the Web, but unfortunately, we also need to *be cautious all of the time.* Everyone we ever engage in a relationship with, whether business or personal, starts as a stranger. We meet strangers every day. People can find us in the phone book, on the Internet, and through our businesses. People can follow us home from anywhere. People have been practicing deceit since long before the advent of the Internet. Just like the other skills covered in this book, these safety procedures can be practiced online but also need to be applied offline in our many face-to-face encounters.

When pursuing any romantic interests, keep in mind the following safety precautions:

* Don't give out any information that will enable someone to physically find you until you are reasonably confident that he or she can be trusted.

* Always meet the first time in a safe, public place in the daytime.

* Be responsible for your own transportation and financial needs.

* Trust your intuition.

* Always tell someone where you have gone and what you know about the person you are meeting.

A woman in her 40s wrote to say she has found a clever way of handling the safety issue of a first meeting. "I always meet in an airport coffee shop—on the other side of the security checks!" Another woman recommends teaming up with a friend for all initial meetings.

Carol, a woman in her 30s, offers this safety-minded protocol: "I never give my number out. If they want to talk, then they have to give me their number and I block my number prior to calling them. It is clear both men and women must be careful, but, for me, being a rather petite, single mother with no family or friends in the area, being too careful is not a downfall."

How soon after an online introduction do you feel it is reasonable to meet in person? What would you need to know or do to feel safe? A little forethought now can save you from an uncomfortable—or dangerous—situation later.

The Next Best Thing to Being There

People say that the telephone is "the next best thing to being there." And, for those dating online, it is definitely a good next step after e-mail introductions. You can tell a lot more from a phone conversation than you can from the written word. Subtle nuances emerge, and in addition to being able to exchange more information, hearing someone's voice gives your intuition more to work with. Voices can be deceptive, though, so you must still use your head. Hearing someone's voice offers more information, but never all the information you need.

One man wrote to say he traveled quite a distance to meet a woman who had a really sexy voice, only to find that her voice and appearance didn't match up. Barbara, a woman in her 40s, said, "No matter how interesting someone is in writing, if I don't like their telephone voice, it is simply not on. I guess I am more shallow than I thought."

On the other hand, the opposite is equally possible. I once did a phone-in radio talk show. A man called to ask me a question and his voice sounded very unstable. The host told him that we would be right back after a commercial break. While the advertising was running, the host said to me, "when we get back on, we'll take the call from Mr. Scary Voice," and then assured me that if the guy turned out to be as weird as he sounded, they would politely disconnect him. As it turned out, the caller was a sincere man with a valid comment. If we had judged him solely on his voice we would have missed a pleasant interaction.

Phone conversations can reveal a lot more than voice quality, however. Remember to practice the skills that you have already learned in terms of asking questions and listening for themes. A person's choice of words is just as important when speaking as when writing—perhaps even more so, as they have not had time to edit.

I have a dear friend, Jeff, who is in the middle of a phone relationship with a woman he has never met. He has shown me pictures of her in which she looks breathtakingly beautiful, and he spends 3 to 5 hours a day on the phone with her long-distance. This kind of time spent talking and sharing is a huge step in the direction of being able to translate the relationship from voice-to-voice to face-to-face. They know they are verbally compatible and that their minds are a successful match. They have practiced intellectual foreplay at length, discussing almost every topic under the sun. They have fallen in love with each other's thoughts and philosophies. They are also in love with their vision of who they hope the other person is. What they need to find out now is whether there will be that spark of chemistry, and that cannot be determined until they meet in person.

▨ **Are you comfortable giving out your phone number? Would you prefer to be called or do the calling? Consider how you'd like to handle this step of the dating process and, if necessary, get voice mail set up to assist you.**

Several of the questions I receive from people seeking dating advice have to do with when to call a potential date, how often to call, and, most especially, wondering after an initial meeting "Why hasn't he/she called when they said they would?" Since everyone's preferences and expectations about these issues vary, *it pays to ask* a potential date what their preferences are before you are in the situation, and to take the time to consider and communicate your own preferences. There is a fine balance between appropriate lavishing of attention on someone you are interested in and appearing desperate and obsessive. Observe yourself, communicate with your potential partner, and choose actions in alignment with your personal code of ethics.

One piece of advice that I can offer for sure is, please don't say you are going to call and then not follow through. It is better to call or e-mail and say that you have decided that you don't want to continue dating than to leave someone hanging out by the phone wondering what went wrong. The second-guessing, analyzing, and confusion that takes place in the wake of a broken promise to call is devastating and unproductive. Consider how you would prefer to be treated, and then consider how you think your date would prefer to be treated. As uncomfortable as honesty may be for you, a little well-placed truth can save your would-be date from hours or even days of frustration.

▓ **How soon after a date do you like to receive or make a follow-up phone call? How often do you think it is appropriate for you to receive or make phone calls to a potential partner? Do you say you'll call when you don't intend to? Would you rather be lied to or told the truth about the likelihood of a second date or follow-up phone call?**

▓ **Make a list of respectful ways that you can let someone know that you aren't interested in continuing to date, without leaving them waiting for that promised phone call.**

The Neutral Zone

If you live far apart, you face a greater challenge than popping over to the local Starbucks to meet your online liaison. So, when you two decide to traverse the miles and meet, how will it work? Should she go to his hometown—his turf—or does he go to hers? Is it safe? What if he's a kook? What if she is a "fatal attraction"? Do you stay in a hotel or accept the offer to stay at your date's house (in the extra bedroom, of course)? Does he pay or does she? Do you let the other person pick you up at the airport and risk getting into a stranger's car? What if you don't like each other? What if you do?! How do you take the next step of meeting *without* all the pressure, vulnerability, and safety issues?

Being dependent on someone else for transportation or a place to stay makes you really vulnerable. Having no other objective for traveling to the meeting place puts a lot of pressure on the relationship, and the money or time spent on the trip adds to the disappointment if it doesn't work out. Knowing someone is in town just to see you when it turns out that you have no interest in spending time with them can also add stress to the situation. Betty wrote me that she went to meet a man in another state. She had booked a room in a hotel so she was independent. "He wanted to spend every second that I was there with me, but I wasn't interested in him after we met. It was pretty awkward."

Linda told this story: "I live in Canada and I met someone online who lives in Northern California. We chatted for a while, exchanged photos, and then talked on the phone. He called me regularly and I began to think this was 'it.' He seemed perfect! He asked me to come to San Francisco to meet him and was very persistent. I'm not fond of traveling so it was a *huge* decision for me to go— especially alone. I was so nervous when the day came. He picked me up at the airport and though he looked older than his pictures, everything else about him seemed true. He kept looking at me and complimenting me, so everything started out really well. The next day, I don't know what happened. He turned to me and said, 'My heart just doesn't beat for you. I don't feel a spark.' That was that. There I was, stuck in California. He didn't even want to drive me back to the airport. I was crushed."

The challenge of long-distance blind dates has led me to coin the phrase "meet in a neutral zone." The neutral zone is turf that doesn't "belong" to either person. One solution is to meet halfway between his turf and hers in place where neither person has "the home court advantage" or the responsibility of playing tour guide. A man on Maui was e-dating a woman on the island of Oahu. Rather than meeting on one or the other person's island, they decided to meet on the island of Lanai for a lunch date.

Workshops, conferences, or retreats also constitute good neutral zone meeting places. They provide you with an additional, satisfying reason for your get-together, as well as an environment that lets you further explore your interests and potential compatibility. They provide not just a neutral zone but a safe "space" for getting to know each other.

If one or both of you are going to have to travel a long distance to meet the other, an interesting option is taking advantage of travel opportunities with other singles that some online dating services are offering. Traveling in an organized group with a potential partner provides an opportunity for finding out whether or not you are a match, and yet, because there are others around, you can easily opt to take things a little bit slower than you might if you were alone.

I have had the honor of participating in international trips for Matchnet Travel with groups of singles from all over the world. My role on these trips has been to teach relationship skills, facilitate the group dynamics, and offer individualized consultation as requested. In doing so, I have discovered how valuable these trips can be for getting to know a potential sweetheart better—*a lot better!* There is no hiding over the course of a week or two. By the end of the trip, everyone's personality traits have been revealed, and many deep and lasting friendships have been established. Some individuals unexpectedly emerge as gems, and compatibility—or lack thereof—becomes clearly established. Sometimes you may have an initial attraction to someone, but after a couple days of being with him or her, you see the situation differently. Other times, giving a person a little time to get comfortable reveals their true nature as a really good catch. On the first day of one of the trips, one of the male travelers asked one of the women if she would go out with him when they returned home. She answered intelligently, "I don't know yet, ask me again in 10 days!"

A lot of the pressure is taken off if you both make it clear that you enjoy traveling and are there to be part of the group, while at the same time getting a clear picture of each other from a new angle. The trip itself provides you with something else to focus on besides the relationship, and if it isn't a match you still have plenty of other things to do. By the same token, there is some safety in numbers, so if your date turns out to be a little "off," or not someone you end up wanting to hang out with, there are other people to spend time with—both for you and for your date. If you and your date are a match, the trip will provide a wonderful experience from which to launch your relationship into the next phase.

■ If you are dating long distance via the Internet, or intend to, think through a plan for meeting in a neutral zone. What ideas do you have for a place to meet that is neither "his" nor "hers"?

■ For a cross-town rendezvous, what would be a good neutral place to meet that is both safe and an appropriate setting for exploring the relationship's potential?

13

From Hard Drive to Sex Drive

"She sent me a card saying to 'keep smiling the beautiful way you do.' We wrote back and forth, sending each other pictures, and building our enthusiasm between Greece and Australia. Finally, 3 months later she was coming to Greece for a holiday. We spoke on the phone, making plans to meet. She said that she liked the way I spoke to her and that I made her feel that 'she was going to meet a very special man.' The rest was up to me to show her who I am.

When I got to the meeting place, my heart was beating so fast and strong. I felt like I was coming close to meeting the most unique person of my life. I searched the square where we were to rendezvous. She was hidden on a bench in the darkest corner watching the sea, expecting me to find her. I looked at her and she looked at me and we were both fulfilled. From 10:00 P.M. until 4:00 A.M., we sat watching the ocean, listening to wonderful music, and talking about ourselves, both feeling a unique attraction from deep love to sexual craziness."

DIMITRI, 36

NOW IS WHEN ALL THIS VIRTUAL FOREPLAY comes to a climax—the moment of meeting. Elements of chemistry, honesty, attraction, safety, excitement, and hope all come together into either one giant crescendo or one big disappointment. When you meet, one of several possibilities will happen. The connection that was felt online will transform into real-life chemistry and a relationship will begin to brew, or the other person will stand you up, or there will be no attraction and tremendous disappointment, or you will become great friends—but not sweethearts. In this chapter, we will explore some of the different realities that affect the transition from online to off.

Donna, a woman in her 30s, was deeply hurt by her experience: "I started talking to this guy who I thought was a prince. He made me feel like he really cared and looked forward to meeting me. I got all dressed up and ended up having lunch by myself. He chickened out." Jerry, a man in his 40s, didn't get off so easily: "I conversed with a wonderful person who fit my every desire. After seeing her picture, I felt she was good-looking, too. I thought I had met the perfect mate, but she was from another state. We discussed her moving here and she was willing. We met and she seemed to be everything I ever wanted in a mate, so I moved her into my home. My God! She was the psycho beast from hell!"

Tony, a 25-year-old man, also had a disappointing date: "A girl traveled 200 miles to meet me. I hadn't seen her picture before we met, but she sounded great on the phone. We met for lunch and she was awful—ugly and immature, and we had so little to talk about. I had to make an excuse about where my car was parked and rush off."

Elizabeth, a woman in her 40s, described her wonderful experience: "We were instantly attracted to each other via e-mail and photos. The night before meeting in person, neither of us could sleep. When I walked into the agreed-upon meeting place, he was already there with roses and a card. I was in shock. The attraction for each other was even stronger in person. We both felt an instant connection."

A 50-year-old gay man told me his unusual story: "I met two men on the Internet: one, Tom, who lived nearby and another, Gary, who lived about a hundred miles away. When Gary came to visit, I introduced them and they fell in love—with each other, leaving me out completely!"

The range of experiences at the moment of meeting is vast. Anything can happen, and just because your partner writes great e-mail or sounds wonderful on the phone doesn't mean that you will feel a stirring of the heart when you meet. One person said that one of the unfortunate things about meeting is that often you have developed a really close virtual friendship, and when you meet, if it isn't a match, you lose not only a sweetheart, but often a friend as well. On the other hand, you may find that your world of wonderful friends expands exponentially, regardless of whether your meeting yields a love match or not.

> ▨ **When meeting your e-date for the first time, keep your hopes up but your mind open.**

Use Your Head, Don't Lose Your Head

Fantasy is a very powerful force, primarily because it is always based on a perfection that doesn't exist in real life. When we fantasize about who our pen pal is, we imagine them without morning breath, without faults, as if they were in a constant state of understanding and empathy with us. Being involved in a long-term fantasy relationship with someone we are never likely to meet can drastically interfere with our real-time relationships. Real people have a hard time competing with the imagined perfection of a fantasy lover.

Your imagination can also severely impact the moment of meeting. When we read a really good book, we visualize what all the characters look like and feel we know them intimately. If we see a movie version of the book, we inevitably feel let down because the characters don't match our internal pictures. If we had seen the movie before reading the book, the movie would have been fine.

Alan, 32, advised: "Meet in person as soon as possible. Don't wait long periods to learn all you can about the other's personality or history; find out if you actually like the way she looks, moves, or talks, first. Otherwise, everything you learned will just cause you pain when you realize you aren't attracted to her and your little imaginary fantasy of her being the perfect person bursts. Meet face-to-face and turn the relationship into a real one as soon as possible."

The more honest and accurate you and your partner are in your verbal communication and descriptions of yourselves, the better the transition from virtual to physical will go for you. Your expectations and what you "deliver" will be in alignment with each other. The mismatch between expectations and the physical world is what causes the problems.

Wendy, 48, said, "People are more complex than their neatly packaged profiles. There's a depth and richness to all of us that can only be hinted at online—and real people don't always match up exactly to our vision of an imaginary dream partner. If we can accept each other as full, not flawless, beings, when we come together we can create something greater than either may have imagined."

The best way to sabotage a face-to-face meeting is to lie about yourself or send false pictures. Jerry, a man in his 40s, was conversing with a woman online when they exchanged pictures. He took a picture with a digital camera and sent the shot 10 minutes later. She chose to send him one of herself at about the age of 40, in a bikini looking quite voluptuous. After talking a bit more, they decided to meet. When he went to the airport to pick her up, a woman in her 50s with gray hair walked up to him. She knew who he was because he looked just like his picture. He didn't recognize her as the woman in the bathing suit, and was quite disappointed. He goes on to explain, "Had she sent me a picture of the way she looked now I may have still been interested, but she misled me, so the picture in my head didn't match the reality."

If you want someone to like you, don't fill them with false images—they are plenty good at that themselves and do not need your help. Instead, honestly love yourself so they can honestly love you, too.

Honor Other Possibilities

Expectations are nasty critters and they extend far beyond what we think someone looks like. We develop expectations about people's personality and character. When our arms are full of expectations, we can't embrace what is available to us. There is no room. If you enter a date with a head full of expectations about the other person and how your relationship will end up, you are bound for disappointment. If you approach it with your arms and heart open to the possibilities—friend, sweetheart, or someone to avoid in the future—one way or another, your expectations will be fulfilled.

Whenever I used to see chocolate, I had an overwhelming urge to eat it. To me, the value was in the taste. I didn't want to indulge myself in this fattening luxury with any regularity, however. One day, as I walked past a chocolate store, I realized that taste was just one of my senses and not the *only sense.* From that moment on, I decided to honor my other senses as well. So now I will walk into a chocolate store to fill my senses of sight and smell and be satisfied without having to actually eat the chocolate.

When you venture out to meet an online pen pal, consider *all* the possible benefits. A love relationship is like taste, taking the other person into your own being so they become part of you. You can, however, embrace other ways of enjoying a meeting. Friendship, a support system, someone to learn from, a business contact—there are many ways to enjoy a new person, beyond fully entwining your lives.

Katie told me that she had had a yearlong friendship with an awesome man she had met online. He lived in Hawaii and she lived on the mainland. She says, "He was absolutely the most romantic, caring, and beautiful person to whom I have ever written. He taught me about myself, life, and how one could live it happily. I met him when I was there on vacation and he was even better in person than I imagined! I will never forget him!" I don't know the details of why they are not together, but this is a fine example of how the experience of knowing someone often outweighs the importance of the longevity or nature of that relationship.

▩ **Open your mind and heart to all the possibilities.**

Chemistry and Attraction

Attraction is not enough to maintain a relationship, yet without the mysterious elements of chemistry and attraction, a relationship is simply a friendship. A solid romantic relationship needs both chemistry and common ground. It requires a connection of head, heart, and body. On the Internet, we have the opportunity to discover whether we have anything in common, but we don't find out about attraction until we meet face-to-face.

What causes chemistry between two people is a complete mystery. A person may be absolutely gorgeous and still not spark your interest. Someone else may be obnoxious and superficially unappealing, but hold some kind of sexual magnetism for you. There is no way to define sexual attraction and no way to dictate it. You can't make chemistry where it isn't, nor can you avoid noticing it when it does exist. Personally, I think this is where that concept of a soul mate enters the picture. People we feel inexplicably drawn to, or who seem familiar to us upon first meeting, are people our souls already know, even though our brains don't.

While the connection between two people is either going to be there or it isn't, there are things that you can do to help make that energy more or less *recognizable*. Basic attraction is affected by our senses. How you put yourself together is more important than how your body is put together.

Kristina said, "I met someone over the Net who seemed like the perfect person for me. He met my every qualification. We spent months e-mailing and having wonderful phone conversations before we ever met. After I met him, I realized this was not someone I could be with, wonderful as he was. To my surprise, he lacked in the area of personal hygiene. He didn't bathe every day and had very bad oral hygiene. Even though this was someone I had become very fond of, I realized that I could never be with him romantically. It was really sad, and it was horrible to have to tell him without hurting his feelings."

If you find you are receiving negative feedback from the dating world, once again, step back and self-observe. Is there anything you can do that would make you a more desirable partner? Think about what people have told you. Is any of it true? Can something be done about the feedback you have received?

> ▨ **Take a personal inventory. Consider all the senses when you**
> **evaluate yourself. How are you putting yourself together**
> **visually? Are your fingernails clean? Are your clothes clean?**
> **How do you smell? How do you sound—what words do you**
> **use and what tone of voice? If you can't see yourself clearly,**
> **ask friends (or professionals) for help.**

A gay man shared with me his first meeting with someone that he had met on the Net: "The first time we met he came straight from work and he was a mess. His clothes were dirty and his breath was horrible. Apparently he had just eaten a garlic pizza or something. I wasn't impressed. I gave him another chance though, and the next time he looked great." First impressions weigh heavily—keep in mind that most people won't give you a second chance.

While all of the above is true for the dating process and first meetings, it actually holds true all the way through a relationship, for years and years on end. Yes, being in a partnership with someone means "for better or for worse, in sickness and in health." But no one wants to marry someone whose positive attitude and good hygiene stop once they're married. Even more important, none of us feels good about ourselves under those circumstances, either.

At the same time, it is completely normal that we will all go through periods of highs and lows, good days and bad days, good years and bad years. And the commitment of partnership helps us get through the rough times. We all have aspects of our being that we would change if we could. In partnerships, we have a responsibility to accept the things we cannot change and strive to be our best on the rest.

One woman wrote, quite dismayed, that the man she had married after a long-distance courtship wasn't turning out to be all that she had hoped: "When we were only seeing each other a couple of times a month, we had sex each time we got together. Now that we're married, however, my husband still only wants sex once or twice a month. I tried everything to get his attention. Now I'm so depressed that I'm completely letting myself go, not even getting dressed or combing my hair." While her frustration is understandable, her choice of responses to the event is certainly not going to bring about the outcome that she is hoping for.

The main point is to self-observe, be aware, and take care of your physical, mental, emotional, and spiritual self—for yourself, if not for your partner. I spoke extensively about self-esteem earlier, but keep in mind that how you feel about yourself and how you treat others will deeply affect how they feel about you, as well.

> **Pay attention to the details. Look your best. Do the best you can with what you have.**

Be What You Seek

Melissa, 42, is a woman who sends me regular e-mail updates about her experiences with online dating. After several very enthusiastic letters about Dean, a guy she had e-mailed for months but had only met briefly in person for a drink, she wrote to announce that they were finally going to spend a whole day together—at the beach. Mixed in with her excitement about spending time with him was concern about her body image and which swimsuit to wear. In spite of the fact that she is quite attractive, Melissa was worried about whether Dean would judge her body harshly since love, in their case, was not yet blind. She overcame her insecurity and wore her favorite bikini.

Looking forward to receiving an e-mail with the details of their day, I was surprised when Melissa wrote back describing a point system she had devised for Dean. He gained points for being handsome and for having nice legs. But he had a bit of a belly, so she "marked him down" for that and then gave him "several points off" for a flat butt, as well. As I read Melissa's e-mail, my mouth dropped open in amazement. I hoped for her sake that Dean didn't do the same thing to her. With a little self-observation, Melissa would have realized that she treated Dean exactly the way she was afraid of being treated.

As you consider what you want in a partner, pay attention also to how you are as a partner. Do not expect to receive more than you are willing to give. If you want someone fit, be someone fit. If you want someone who doesn't drink or abuse substances, be someone who doesn't do those things. I have a friend who wanted her husband to stop drinking because she felt he was an alcoholic, but she wasn't willing to give up wine with dinner herself. If you want someone who is kind, considerate, and non-judgmental, start by being those things.

> **This is the time and place to apply all the ways that you have grown and all the skills you have gained by dating online. Let your true self shine.**

Stretch your definition of who you are. If online dating made you more outgoing, be more outgoing when face-to-face. If you took little risks by sharing your heart with someone online, share your heart in person. If online dating made you more confident, be more confident in person. If you were a good communicator in e-mail, be a good communicator in person. If you were better able to define what you wanted in a partner based on your experiences on the Net, hold on to those qualifications. If you learned you don't have to settle for less than you want, don't. If you discovered that you like who you are, be that! If you were able to access these aspects of your personality on the Net, you have it in you! You can do it. You can be it. Stretch!

Taking It All the Way

Marisa, an 18-year-old, says, "Cyber sex is not sex. It may appear to be in a sense, but you really have to know the difference between reality and fantasy." The same is true of relationships. While on the Net, you can build a great foundation for a potential relationship, but in order to have a connection of body, mind, and soul, you have to get face-to-face to see what happens. If the intellectual and virtual foreplay that you have experienced with a partner online leads you to believe you have an alignment of head and heart, the remaining element is the physical.

While the following discussion is geared toward those who have already made the decision to be—or are considering being—physically intimate with an online liaison, the questions of *when* and *if* cannot be overlooked. The obvious issues of personal morality, physical and emotional safety, sexually transmitted diseases, and the potential of creating a new life with this cyber stranger must be taken into serious consideration. The key is, once again, to know yourself and identify your values, consider your goals, and choose actions that are in alignment with who you are, what you want, and your personal code of ethics.

While asking questions, discussing sexuality, or even sharing sexual fantasies online may reveal a lot of information or build a certain level of sexual desire, when it comes to sex there is no replacement for the real thing. No matter what you say in e-mail or chats, no words can replace a long lingering look into your lover's eyes, a hug, a kiss, and body-to-body contact.

In addition, the ability to write about sex or even talk about sex doesn't necessarily translate to sexual fulfillment in person. One woman pointed out, however, that while having cyber sex "You can actually learn a lot to add to your relationship in regard to the bedroom." The same holds true for any discussion related to sex; you can take what you learn about your own and the other person's sexuality and apply it. We are often uncomfortable telling another person what we like and don't like sexually. Instead, we keep hoping that he or she will find the right spot or touch us in a different way. However, an honest discussion can serve the valuable purpose of defining boundaries, expectations, and desires and can lead to a rich and fulfilling sex life.

Remember the skills you have learned so far in this book also apply here. Self-observe, use "I" statements, and take responsibility for your feelings. A statement such as "I like to be kissed slowly and passionately" is a lot easier to hear and offers more to work with than "You don't kiss the way I would like you to." The first mode of communicating would likely make your partner want to try your suggestion, while the second would likely hurt them and push them away. No one wants to "miss the mark," so to speak. And simply showing your partner what you like and how you like it beats by a long shot years of wishing they knew!

Intellectual Foreplay dedicates a chapter to questions about sex and sexual preferences for you to explore with a potential partner. Here are a few for you to play with before, or perhaps after, you and your partner move toward the bedroom:

* How do you like to be kissed? How important is kissing to you?

* How do you feel about sex before marriage? What are your personal morals and ethics?

* How much or what kind of foreplay do you prefer? Is there anything you don't like during the foreplay stage of lovemaking (such as ear kissing, direct genital touching, et cetera)?

✳ Is there anything that must be included in foreplay or lovemaking for you to be really aroused (such as kissing, talking, direct touching, ear kissing, eye gazing, et cetera)?

✳ Do you prefer that the lights are on or off while you make love?

✳ Do you have a favorite place for making love? Where?

✳ Are you interested in having sex in different or unusual places (such as outside, in the car, on the beach)?

There is a fair amount of communication, negotiation, and compromise that can be required when people are exploring their sexuality. Since sexuality is such an intimate and vulnerable arena, being open to the other's wishes, while at the same time honoring and respecting comfort levels and boundaries, are also key elements. By thinking through your own answers to questions about sexuality first you'll know your own boundaries and interests more thoroughly, and will be better able to share them and stick to them when you're with someone else.

One of the dynamics that people face when they transition their online relationship to offline is the sensation that they know someone intimately already, which could cause them to become sexually involved more quickly than they would normally. We tend not to take the same time to get to know someone in person when we've had a lot of time for anticipation to build up. Sexuality quickly gets misidentified as the only uncharted territory after a long verbal courtship.

Tori, 45, shared with me her conviction that she wasn't going to have sex the first time she met the man with whom she was having a long-distance courtship: "I don't want him to think I'm easy, so I'm going to be strong and say 'no.'" However, the intimacy that they had created through writing and talking on the phone quickly translated to their face-to-face relationship when they met. She called me a day later to tell me that she and her online friend were now lovers. While she was quite happy about it, she was also concerned that there wasn't a real foundation beneath this very intimate start to their relationship. Without that foundation, everything moves along fine until an earthquake rocks your world and the relationship doesn't have the depth or strength to hold up through conflict and problem solving.

Tina, a woman in Germany, wrote to tell me about her first meeting with her online man in the United States: "Remember how nervous I was before flying to the United States to meet my online friend? I'm happy to tell you that everything worked out just great. When I walked off the plane, I took a deep breath just like you advised, and the ice was broken after only a few minutes. I guess we've been talking so much on the instant messenger that is wasn't all that hard getting used to each other. I can safely say that we hit it off and fell for each other head over heels. You can imagine how hard it was to leave again after spending 2 weeks together."

Tina sent me an update a month later saying, "We talk more than couples who are actually together. Our conversations are very intense and sometimes we spend hours talking about anything. I've never been so open with another person. We both bought Webcams so we can see each other—which is quite an experience. Of course, now we want to be together even more."

Webcams have quickly become an intermediary step between writing online and being together physically. In addition to being able to see each other typing, couples are having sex—separated by their computers and Webcams, trying to bridge the gap between the virtual and physical worlds.

Unfortunately, the intimacy that is created online doesn't always translate to the bedroom. Walt, 43, was shocked to find that the person he'd thought of as a potential partner was the furthest thing from it: "I met this one woman for the weekend whom I had been talking to for a while online. She turned out to be unattractive, vulgar, and wanted to make love immediately—practically in front of her children. There's no kind or gentlemanly way to tell someone they are hideous and that you'd prefer to douse yourself with napalm rather than even contemplate making love to them!"

My friend Jeff, whom I mentioned in the last chapter, finally went to meet the woman he'd been corresponding with for months. They hit it off right away and spent their 2 weeks together making love several times a day. When I asked him about the relationship upon his return, he said she was wonderful, but that the "spark" was missing and he didn't know how to tell her. At this point, it was the woman my heart went out to, as she didn't know he felt that way and had given herself completely in the hopes that their relationship was going to blossom into something permanent. Spending that 2 weeks exploring their face-to-face relationship to see if the spark was there before mixing sex into the whole thing would have, undoubtedly, minimized the pain that she went through when he broke the news to her.

▨ **Take your time. When you first meet your online love, allow yourselves time to see if the shell of intimacy and trust you created online can be filled with true trust and intimacy in person. Refer to your personal code of ethics and hold yourself to the same standards and values as you would if you were meeting the person for the very first time—because, in essence, you are.**

Respectfully Yours

As a relationship specialist, many people ask my opinion of what is right and wrong sexual expression, as they try to define their own levels of willingness and acceptance. I always explain that there is no clear definition when it comes to consensual sex. "Right" and "wrong" are defined by the morals of the people participating, not by experts, ministers, or friends. Sexuality isn't a right and wrong issue—it is a *respect* issue. If something is right for you and wrong for the other person, then trying to impose your way on the other is not respectful and, therefore, not right.

A beautiful woman in her early 30s, Angelina, told me about her situation. She explained, "I am still a virgin waiting for marriage, but my boyfriend is not. He is trying to be respectful of my pace, but it is hard for him." Any of us can empathize with the challenge two such different levels of sexual readiness or experience can cause, but this wasn't their real problem. She said, "He told me that if we got married, he would want me to do all this kinky stuff," and went on to describe a variety of sexual practices that are more the extreme than the norm. He wanted her to get breast implants and acrylic nails, dress in revealing clothing, and occasionally act as a dominatrix in some S&M play. I looked at this sweet, innocent, churchgoing, woman in amazement as she described what this man was asking her to do. I thought of all the women who already match what he was looking for and wondered why he would want to transform Angelina into something so far from her natural self.

Searching for understanding, she asked me, "Is that normal?" I took a deep breath, resisting my inclination to tell her to run as fast as she could from a man who showed her no respect, who caused her to doubt her own beauty, style, readiness, and morals. Instead, I said, "It is normal for him, but it isn't normal for you—and *that* is what is relevant."

Sexuality is a matter of honor and respect. The goal is to share feeling wonderful, beautiful, celebrated, loved, touched, adored, ecstatic, and fulfilled. If only one person is feeling any combination of these, while the other is not, then respect and honor are missing. Both partners must have respect for themselves as well as for each other. Experimenting and stretching your sexual interests and activities can be wonderful, but when you get out of bed in the morning, your self-respect must still be intact.

Know, honor, and communicate your personal boundaries.

The very nature of our language of love has contributed to our problems in this realm. In our society, when we refer to having sex, we say we are making love *to* someone. I maintain that we don't make love *to,* but *with,* another person. If we simply were to change our words and the mind-set that accompanies them, a whole shift in the way we make love could take place. By exploring and honoring each other's desires, interests, and boundaries, we truly make love *together,* rather than *to* each other.

> 🀫 **Pay attention to the language you use when thinking or talking about sex. Do your words carry the meaning that you want to create? Shift your words to align with your heart.**

Ken, a 45-year-old man, had his own personal website in which he clearly defined the kind of intimacy he was looking for: "Do you ever long to be dreamy and intoxicated, kissing deeply—seeming to devour each other completely and feeling as one...a slow symphony of hands and dreamy eyes having hours to play. A hot passion, but one that is under control, not animal-like. Dreamy soulful eyes, moans, hands exploring and worshiping while a powerful erotic electricity is skillfully, leisurely, and playfully built up to unbearable levels. Then I'm finally inside you, making gentle, slow, passionate love—not just sex. We breathe the same breath, we merge, our souls are one, we feel what the other is feeling, and our whole body is erotically charged. Just on the edge and leisurely teasing each other, playing blissfully for hours. When we finally climax together, though, it is scary, because the powerful, erotic charge we cultivated seems to open and surrender parts of our heart further, parts of our heart never opened and touched until now. We can't help it, so we cry—this is the depth of passion and spiritual connection we always wanted! The holes in our hearts and souls seem to slowly heal. We lay quivering, then giggling in delight, and drift off to sleep together for a while with me still deep inside you. Still buzzing and smiling for a couple days. Best of all, we have enough other values and interests in common to be soul mates for life. We like to do what it takes to learn to have a great relationship so that our chemistry won't fade much through our many years together. This never-ending goal of being able to master an intimate relationship flows naturally from something we have in common—a broader interest in personal growth. But there is much more to relationships than soulful love, so please put this aside and get to know the rest of me—the normal way—as a dear friend."

14

Happily Ever After

SO, YOU'VE MET YOUR PERFECT MATCH. He or she is everything you've every dreamed of—or pretty close to it. How do you go from finding each other to happily ever after? How are you going to keep your partnership from becoming another statistic on the "relationships gone bad" list? Keeping love alive requires maintenance. Just like a garden, you have to nourish love and give it your time. If you don't keep paying attention, monitoring and encouraging love, the weeds of negligence, intolerance, and indifference will grow...and the love will die.

When transitioning from the virtual to the real world, you really have to start fresh and build a new relationship based on who your partner is, rather than who you think they are. You have the benefit, however, of an already established friendship.

When Steven and I met, we spent a week together in person and then 5 months on the phone with only two weekend visits. I remember so clearly when he came to pick me up at the airport the day I moved to Maui. I looked across the front seat of his truck at this man whom I knew so much about, had shared hundreds of hours with talking on the phone, and yet who was almost a total stranger. I had a hard time matching the man I was looking at with the one whose voice I knew so well. All kinds of mixed emotions were welling up within me. I had quit my job, left my family, and moved, for all purposes, to another planet—all to be with this man whom I knew intimately verbally, but knew very little physically.

When you fall in love online or over the phone, you fall in love with communication. You fall in love with ideas and concepts and an intermingling of words. When you are face-to-face sharing time together, suddenly the focus of the conversation shifts from heartfelt theories of life and intimate musings of the soul to "what do you want for dinner?" If you ignore it, the contrast of this transition can be devastating. Says one 21-year-old woman, "You can get so used to expressing your feelings online that you cannot express them properly in a real relationship." To build a relationship on this kind of communication and then to stop cold when you transition to being together in person can be jolting.

> ▓ **Let the Internet be practice and continue to express yourself face-to-face.** Make a conscious effort to keep communicating about the things that matter to you, that intrigue you, that stir your soul, pique your curiosity, or cause you to wonder.

If you wrote romantic poetry to each other, continue to do so. If you sent each other beautiful pictures of places you dreamt of going, continue to dream, share, and imagine in person. Let your maturing relationship also be a process of exploration. If you think you know everything your partner thinks, imagines, and cares about without asking, listening, and discovering, you will eventually take them for granted. Continue practicing the intellectual foreplay that got you into the relationship. Just because you have consummated your relationship doesn't mean that the foreplay should stop!

> ▓ **Dating in person or living together doesn't mean the romance of the written word has to stop. Continue to send each other e-mail. Leave love messages on sticky notes around the house. Make time in real life for the kinds of conversations that you shared on the Net.**

Think Before You Speak

One of the advantages of online communication that you lose in a face-to-face relationship is the opportunity to think carefully about how you want to respond to something. Online, you can write your note, reread it, edit it, and perhaps consult your friends before sending the message. In real life we aren't afforded that much opportunity to think before we speak. Certain elements of the online kind of conscious communication, however, are extremely valuable in a relationship, especially when dealing with challenging issues.

Before you respond to something your partner says that upsets you, stop and self-observe. What are you feeling? Are you hurt? Are you afraid? Are you taking responsibility? Think before you speak and take responsibility for how you are feeling. By doing this, you will be able to *choose* your response rather than react unconsciously. Unconscious words and comments that we use in relationships are often what end up killing the love, one word at a time. Remember to apply the skills you have been practicing, such as E + R = OS, using "I" statements, and avoiding the blame game.

By reading *Virtual Foreplay*, you have become aware of the strengths that you have gained by dating online. You have also undoubtedly added a few more skills to your repertoire for enhancing your self-esteem, communicating with others, and taking personal responsibility for what you are creating. By examining what you have already done, you will be able to apply this same process to building, maintaining, and repairing your real-life relationships.

Let's review the process. You have now:

1. determined whether you are ready and willing to be in a relationship

2. asked yourself some challenging self-assessment questions to define who you are, what you want, and what you have to offer

3. taken an active role in honoring yourself and raising your self-esteem

4. determined your personal code of ethics and aligned your behavior with it

5. practiced self-observation

6. shared your thoughts, feelings, interests, and desires thoughtfully and honestly with others

7. taken responsibility for your responses to the events and people in your life

8. discovered your boundaries and learned to say "no thank you" to people and activities that aren't in alignment with your values

9. given your time and attention to relationship building

10. held on to your vision, realigning with your goals if you got off course

11. practiced conscious acts of kindness, brightening other people's lives along your way

12. used your head, trusted your heart, and honored your intuition

Following this twelve-step process will help you not only find love, but also *stay* in love. The application of these steps is obviously far wider than just finding a love partner. *All* your relationships—whether with yourself, a romantic interest, family members, or business associates—can be enhanced by continuing on this path.

The Gift of Time

Dating online requires a time commitment. How much time did you spend on your computer reading profiles, answering e-mail, or hanging out in chats as you searched for your partner? As you transform your relationship from virtual to physical, remember that the relationship still requires your time. Be sure to transfer the time that you spent online to time spent together in real life. Several people told me about 4- to 8-hour dialogs that they carried on with a new love interest online or on the phone. While this kind of time will eventually become unreasonable to spend in person, remember that relationships need some undivided attention. If you get totally wrapped up in work, children, and household chores and don't dedicate any time to romantic maintenance, your relationship risks a slow death.

With romantic interest just a mouse click away on the Internet, be sure to give your partner some loving attention—outside of the bedroom. Don't forget the value of *relationship* foreplay, virtual or intellectual. More goes into romantic readiness than touch. If you indeed met on the Net, remember that your initial interest in each other was in sharing yourselves and listening to each other. Honoring your partner's feelings, listening to them, and cherishing them all go into creating the mood to get physically intimate.

▦ Give yourselves the gift of time.

As you begin the process of creating a home or life together, discuss how you want to handle household duties, financial management, and other concerns of daily life. If you need help with this, *Intellectual Foreplay* has questions on every aspect of combining your daily lives, from time management to yard care. By paying attention to making choices that you both agree on, you will be able to develop a compatible way of handling these realities.

Household duties and job responsibilities have a way of taking over our lives, leaving little room for anything else. As you build or maintain your relationship, consider the interactions that caused you to become interested in each other in the first place. Did you fall in love over sharing your hearts in communication? Did you fall in love talking about things that you enjoy in common, such as camping, bike riding, traveling, or reading? As you transition your relationship from virtual to physical, special attention is required to incorporate the things that initially drew you together.

Recreation or playtime is also an important part of keeping a relationship alive. The word "recreation" breaks into "re-creation": "to create again." The *American Heritage Dictionary's* definition is "refreshment of one's mind or body after work through activity that amuses or stimulates, play." If you want to re-create your love or stimulate your relationship, give your relationship time away from all the stresses of everyday life. Don't wait for a vacation once a year. Take mini-vacations that may last from as little as a couple hours to a weekend.

> **Now is when you get to do the things you wrote about, the things that you both love—together!**

Keep Learning

My parents are about to celebrate their fiftieth wedding anniversary. As I watch them interact, I realize that one of the things that has kept them interesting to each other is their continuous growth. They are constantly learning, reading, taking classes, and exploring new concepts. For 50 years they have been communicating and yet they continue to discuss new topics, to teach each other what they have learned, and to have fascinating conversations as they make sense of the new subjects that they have encountered. As my mom says, "Spirituality, sexuality, education, communication, and humor, what more do you need?"

> **The key to keeping a relationship interesting is to keep life interesting. Keep learning and share what you discover.**

PART SIX

Love Is a Universal Language

"It restores my faith in mankind to know that there are some really neat people in the world who are also single and searching."
CHERIE, 44

"Variety and diversity encountered from online communication with any and all global cultures educates and elevates individual and human consciousness. Global consciousness is an entity in itself and it is necessary to elevate it, and become one, if we are to save the planet and the human race."
FRANK, 48

"The initial mystery is great, really getting to know someone without being influenced by the package they came in."
ANNA, 52

"It is so sad to see how many millions of visitors are only going to the cyber sex sites on the Internet and not the healthy sites that feed the spirit."
RAYMOND, 48

15

Making the Net Work

ARY SAYS, "I met one of my best friends dating online, and while there are no romantic feelings, I know I can talk to him about anything. We've known each other for about 6 years now and have met in person about five times. We never really clicked romantically, but we are great friends." Another woman in her 50s said, "I have found friendships online with people who I may never meet face-to-face, but they have enriched my life."

Have you ever moved someplace because of a job or to be with a romantic interest, only to find out that the real value of your move was something other than your original reason? Maybe you met someone or experienced a life-changing event that never would have happened if you hadn't moved? This has happened time and time again in my own life; the benefit I think I will gain by a certain decision is replaced with a different, sometimes greater, benefit.

Online dating is much the same. As you explore the Net, hold open the possibility that the reason you are putting yourself on the line may be greater than you first imagined. You may think it is to find a love match, but it could be more far-reaching than that, from developing new interpersonal skills and confidence to making world-wide contacts that may change your life.

International Foreplay

Cynthia met a man in India with whom she felt a deep connection: "We have the freedom to express ourselves without any risk, because we know we will never meet. Being so open has built up a great respect for each other and a deep friendship. We think we will meet someday when we are old and gray, after years of being each other's constant, each other's confidant, each other's lifelong friend."

One of the most fascinating developments that has come out of online dating is the connection of people across borders. Thousands of people are crossing international, political, and racial boundaries daily through the out-of-body travel of e-mail. I have developed contacts, friendships, and business associations from the island of Maui to Long Island, New York, to the island of Mauritius off the coast of Africa, to the Greek islands. Island-to-island contact between all of these distant places would never have happened without the Internet and, specifically, my interest in the online dating phenomenon. What an amazing opportunity we have, literally at our fingertips, for international communication and greater understanding.

Not all that long ago, political divisions cut off information about people and places, such as Russia during the Cold War. We knew very little about each other and, thus, were fearful. Now the Internet enables us to access information about other countries and follow their news. We can talk directly with people in other countries, sharing our hearts and souls, and even our cyber bodies. People are flying to foreign countries to find spouses; our children are mixtures of multiple cultures. We are members of an incredible expanding global society.

Karen, a 28-year-old, says, "With online dating you have a chance to extend the limited circle of your communication (the same people, the same colleagues, the same bars) to search for your match all over the world." A woman in her 40s concurs: "Online dating gives you a wide range of people and places to check out, and in the process you end up learning more about them. For instance, I was writing to someone in Switzerland. I have never been there, so it was fun to learn more about the country and to see photos that were on a more personal basis than in the books." Alex, a man in his 30s, says, "I have friends in many different countries. I know women in Russia, Croatia, England, Singapore, China, the Philippines, Ireland, and Australia. I love learning about different cultures, exchanging different ideals, thoughts, and feelings. I try hard to be honest and a good listener."

Stan, a man in his late 40s, explains, "To learn more about local or international relationships opens our minds to other cultures. We have an opportunity to learn aspects of different languages and become familiar with the way people express themselves. By connecting online we become aware that we are not alone, that there is a wonderful world of people out there. We can become more fraternal as human beings worldwide, experiencing a communion through the virtual world." Of course, true love is also bridging the distances between us.

A Giant Sandbox for Adults

As we've already established, people are finding that they like the Internet as a means of communication because they are freer to share themselves truthfully. This freedom of sharing oneself and being accepted is what we hunger for in our lives. In order to transition this freedom of sharing ourselves to all our daily interactions, we have to practice acceptance—*acceptance of differences.*

Acceptance is another skill that we can practice online—where it is easy—and apply offline—where it really counts. As we encounter people online and develop intimate friendships, without pictures, we are unencumbered by things like skin color, age, or gender; these are unnoticeable and, we begin to realize, unimportant. We can "fall in love" online or have a meeting of the minds as easily with someone from another country or of another color as someone of our own nationality or ethnic background, without even knowing it.

In a workshop I attended, I learned of a study that showed if you put a group of young children of different ethnic backgrounds into a sandbox together they will get along just fine. They don't see color. It is not until they are taught prejudice that they begin to discriminate and judge based on color or ethnicity. In order to teach acceptance and compassion, instead of prejudice, we have to live it, and we can practice that on the Internet. *The Internet is a giant sandbox for adults!*

When you are chatting online, age, gender, financial status, sexual orientation, and racial differentiations are removed. You don't know who you are really talking to and your liking or not liking the other person has nothing to do with these issues. Not until we see a person, hear their voice, or listen to a description of them do we *choose* to exercise our prejudices. Love is a universal language. Love has no color, gender, or age. Love doesn't have a religion. While we may carefully choose a life partner based on the things we have in common, we can have a much broader base of acceptance for people we cherish as friends and associates.

This acceptance needs to extend to male-female interactions, as well. Men and women are not the same critters. We think differently. We have different approaches to life and different styles of communication. However, we seem to be connecting on the Internet. Here, we are speaking our minds, sharing our feelings, establishing our boundaries, sharing our similarities, and acknowledging our differences. What if we were to do the same thing in person, in our relationships—in our "*real*ationships"?!

> What would happen to our planet if we practiced nonjudgmental acceptance on the Internet and then applied this acceptance in our communities and neighborhoods? What if we expanded our capacity to love? We can transform the "lonely planet"!

Six Degrees of Separation

The "Six Degrees of Separation" theory suggests that only five people separate us from any other person on the planet. For instance, say I want to meet the Dalai Lama. My sister knows Jim, who knows Carl, who knows Leslie, who knows Berny, who knows the Dalai Lama. I am, therefore, only separated from the Dalai Lama by five other people—he would be the sixth person.

When you consider this theory in terms of online dating, the benefits of being online expand greatly. If handled properly, it works like a network-marketing model of finding your soul mate! Rather than thinking that you are only connecting with the people you meet online, consider that your perfect match might be the best friend of the man or woman you have been talking to online!

What if we started a different approach to online dating, one in which we served as matchmakers for each other? If you see a man online who sounds wonderful, but who lives in Toronto, let your friend in Toronto know about him. If you meet a special woman online but find she is looking for someone different, help connect her with a man you know who might be a match. Have you ever played the card game *Concentration?* To play, you turn all fifty-two cards over so you can't see their face values. Then, you turn two over, trying to find a matched pair. If they don't match, you return them to their face-down position, but you try to remember what they are and where they are placed, so you can find their match later as you continue turning cards over.

Online dating can be approached in very much the same way. As you read through people's profiles, pay attention to people who sound outstanding but are perhaps not right *for you* or are geographically undesirable *for you*. Then, pass on their profile listing to someone who might be right for them.

What if...

What if the real reason that you are online isn't just to find your soul mate, but rather to reconnect with your own soul, your passion, your vision, and share it with the world? What if the person you met online wasn't supposed to be your mate but rather was the person who knew about a cure for an ailment your mother has? What if, because you posted your profile online, a headhunter from your dream job contacted you? What if someone saw your profile, which revealed your life purpose and aspirations, and called you with the perfect contact to help you make your dream come true?

🔲 **What is the best-case scenario possible for sharing your dreams and visions—your skills, strengths, and interests—with the world?**

What if we logged on to the Internet looking to learn, grow, meet new people, network, help each other, show compassion, make dreams come true, stretch our personalities, gain skills, become better friends and lovers, learn about the world, and expand our capacity to accept differences, take responsibility, and to love. *What if all of that was the virtual foreplay to finding our soul mate online?!*

God bless you on your journey. Remember to trust the process, breathe deeply, love intently, and laugh joyfully along the way!

About the Author

Eve Eschner Hogan, M.A., is an inspirational speaker, educator, and online relationship advisor for AmericanSingles.com, JDate.com, Relationship-Talk.com, AskEveAdvice.com, and the "Wizard of the Dating Realm" for WZ.com. In addition to *Virtual Foreplay*, she is the author of *Intellectual Foreplay: Questions for Lovers and Lovers-To-Be, The Way of the Winding Path,* and coauthor of *Rings of Truth.* Eve is also the Director of Education and Training for Motivating the Teen Spirit, teaching teenagers how to love and respect themselves and to make integrity-based decisions.

Eve has a contagious enthusiasm and a charismatic ability to inspire. She is founder of Wings to Wisdom, www.HeartPath.com, which offers self-mastery seminars helping thousands of people to discover their inner resources, thus expanding their awareness and strengthening their life skills. Eve's specialty is in relationship enhancement, whether the relationship is with yourself, your sweetheart, your family, or with God. She lives on the island of Maui with her husband, Steve, where she also serves as a labyrinth facilitator and wedding officiant.

For more information about Eve, see:

* www.HeartPath.com for articles; seminar schedules; labyrinth, wedding, and book information
* www.EveHogan.com for information about booking Eve as a speaker at your next event
* www.AskEveAdvice.com for personalized advice
* www.VoiceAVision.com for posting a personal prayer or vision

Wings to Wisdom LLC
PO Box 943
Puunene Maui HI 96784
EveHogan@aol.com
(808) 879-8648 * (888) 551-5006

Other Books by Eve Eschner Hogan, M.A.

Intellectual Foreplay: Questions for Lovers and Lovers-to-Be
$13.95, Hunter House Publishers, February 2000

People often choose their romantic partners by "looks good" or "feels good," only to wake up in relationships that really *aren't* good! We even tend to ask more questions about a car that we are buying than about a person we are considering as a life partner or parent to our children. *Intellectual Foreplay* will guide you to ask the right questions, make the right choices, and avoid the wrong partners! *Intellectual Foreplay* is the perfect compliment to *Virtual Foreplay* for exploring relationships online and off!

Rings of Truth
By Jim Britt with Eve Eschner Hogan
$12.95, Health Communications Inc., November 1999

Rings of Truth is a novel in the genre of visionary fiction in which an ethereal woman, Alea, guides both the main character and the readers to discover the keys to letting go of control and approval issues and gain a deep sense of resourcefulness in their lives.

The Way of the Winding Path: A Map to the Spiritual Journey of Life.
(To be released in 2002, White Cloud Press)

The Way of the Winding Path reveals lessons gained from walking the labyrinth, a beautiful, 13th century pattern that is tiled into the floor of the Chartres Cathedral in France. This book leads the reader on the mystical journey of life guided by this metaphorical pilgrimage.

EXTENDED MASSIVE ORGASM: How You Can Give and Receive Intense Sexual Pleasure
by Steve Bodansky, Ph.D., & Vera Bodansky, Ph.D.

Yes, extended massive orgasms can be achieved! In this hands-on guide, Steve Bodansky and his wife Vera describe how to take the experience of sex to a new level of enjoyment. Focusing primarily on women but addressing the needs of men as well, the authors disclose knowledge that is practically unknown except to specialized researchers and involves the stimulation of specific and uniquely sensitive areas. They recommend the best positions for orgasm and offer strategic advice for every technique from seduction to kissing. No matter how long a couple has been together, it's never too late—or too early—to make each other ecstatic in the bedroom. The Bodanskys explain how.

224 pp. 6 illus. 12 b/w photos ... Paperback $14.95

THE POCKET BOOK OF FOREPLAY *by* Richard Craze

Foreplay isn't just a prelude to the "real thing"—it's an experience to be savored for itself. This book shows you how, with full-color pictures providing a guided tour of foreplay, from "Setting the Scene" to "Reaching the Limits."
　　Ever wanted to try foreplay at the office or fantasized about those sexy Tantric techniques? The full range of foreplay fun is here, adding an erotic new dimension to your lovemaking experience. When your relationship falls into a boring routine, instead of looking for another lover try experimenting with foreplay to put the excitement back into your life.

96 pp. ... 68 color photos ... Paperback $10.95

COMING in October 2001
THE POCKET BOOK OF SEX AND CHOCOLATE
　　What more could a body want?

ORDER FORM

10%   DISCOUNT on orders of $50 or more —
20%   DISCOUNT on orders of $150 or more —
30%   DISCOUNT on orders of $500 or more —
On cost of books for fully prepaid orders

NAME _____

ADDRESS' _____

CITY/STATE _____ ZIP/POSTCODE _____

PHONE _____ COUNTRY (outside of U.S.) _____

TITLE	QTY	PRICE	TOTAL
Virtual Foreplay (paper)		@ $13.95	

Prices subject to change without notice

Please list other titles below:

_____		@ $	
_____		@ $	
_____		@ $	
_____		@ $	
_____		@ $	
_____		@ $	
_____		@ $	
_____		@ $	

Check here to receive our book catalog ❏   free

Shipping Costs

First book: $3.00 by bookpost, $4.50 by UPS, Priority Mail, or to ship outside the U.S. Each additional book: $1.00
For rush orders and bulk shipments call us at (800) 266-5592

TOTAL _____

Less discount @ _____ %   (_____)

TOTAL COST OF BOOKS _____

Calif. residents add sales tax _____

Shipping & handling _____

TOTAL ENCLOSED _____

Please pay in U.S. funds only

❏ Check ❏ Money Order ❏ Visa ❏ MasterCard ❏ Discover

Card # _____ Exp. date _____

Signature _____

Complete and mail to:
Hunter House Inc., Publishers
PO Box 2914, Alameda CA 94501-0914
Phone (510) 865-5282 Fax (510) 865-4295
Orders: (800) 266-5592 or www.hunterhouse.com
email: ordering@hunterhouse.com

VFP-6/2001